BASEBALL HAIKU

BASEBALL HAIKU

American and Japanese
Haiku and Senryu on Baseball

Edited with Translations by
Cor van den Heuvel & Nanae Tamura

W. W. Norton & Company   *New York • London*

Copyright © 2007 by Cor van den Heuvel

Manufacturing by R. R. Donnelley, Bloomsburg Division

The acknowledgments, on pp. 207–214, are an extension of this copyright page.

The three haiku by Jack Kerouac (two in the American Baseball Haiku & Senryu section & one on football quoted in the introduction) are from *Book of Haikus* by Jack Kerouac, edited by Regina Weinreich, copyright © 2003 by the Estate of Stella Kerouac, John Sampas, Literary Representative. Used by permission of Penguin, a division of Penguin Group (USA) Inc.

The prose excerpts by Edward J. Rielly quoted in the introduction are from "Baseball Haiku: Bashō, the Babe, and the Great Japanese-American Trade," by Edward J. Rielly. From *The Cooperstown Symposium on Baseball and American Culture, 2001,* copyright © 2002 State University of New York, College at Oneonta, edited by William M. Simons, permission of McFarland & Company, Inc., Box 611, Jefferson, NC 28640. www.mcfarlandpub.com

Library of Congress Cataloging-in-Publication Data

Baseball haiku : American and Japanese haiku and senryu on baseball / Edited with translations by Cor van den Heuvel and Nanae Tamura.
   p. cm.
  ISBN 13: 978-0-393-06219-9
  ISBN-10: 0-393-06219-8
   1. Haiku, American. 2. Baseball—Poetry. 3. Haiku. 4. Senryu. I. Van den Heuvel, Cor, 1931– II. Tamura, Nanae.

PS593. H3B37 2007
811'.04108357—dc22   2007061179

W. W. Norton & Company, Inc., 500 Fifth Avenue, New York, N.Y. 10110
www.wwnorton.com

W. W. Norton & Company, Ltd., Castle House, 75/76 Wells Street, London
W1T 3QT

1 2 3 4 5 6 7 8 9 0

To Masaoka Shiki

Some Special Thank Yous

The editors would like to thank the following: William J. Higginson for help with several learned matters; Hiroaki Sato for finding a number of *naitā* baseball haiku for us and for sharing his knowledge of the present state of haiku and *senryu* in Japan; Emiko Miyashita for finding the baseball haiku by Arima Akito, her *sensei,* and several others; Shunichi Shibota for passing on to us the Taki Shun'ichi "briefcase" haiku; Hoshino Tsunehiko for help with finding baseball haiku, including his own; Yuko Otomo for reading through Kaneko Tohta's collected haiku looking for baseball haiku (there were none); and thanks to all our friends who were on the lookout for baseball haiku, whether they were able to find any or not.

Nanae Tamura would particularly like to thank both the Museum of Haiku Literature in Tokyo and the Shiki-Kinen Museum in Matsuyama for their kind guidance and great help; also Keiko Kawano for finding the baseball haiku of Imai Sei, her haiku teacher; and Tōru Kiuchi, the chief editor of the haiku magazine *Ten* (*Marten*), for checking all the haiku by Ozawa Seiyūshi.

Note on Japanese Names: Except for editor Nanae Tamura's name and some of the names in the above "thank you," all the names of Japanese in this book are (or should be) printed in the Japanese manner, family name first. This includes the names listed in the "Book List," but not the names of Japanese-American authors nor those of Japanese authors when they are mentioned in the book titles or descriptions, if the book was published with their names printed in the Western manner.

The Score Card

Japanese Baseball Haiku

Extra Innings

INTRODUCTION: Warming Up

Baseball Haiku presents more than two hundred of the best haiku about baseball ever written by American and Japanese poets. Haiku and baseball were made for each other: While haiku give us moments in which nature is linked to human nature, baseball is played in the midst of the natural elements—on a field under an open sky; and as haiku happen in a timeless *now,* so does baseball, for there is no clock ticking in a baseball game—the game's not over until the last out.

The few words of a haiku can bring to life a pitcher rotating the ball behind his back as he looks in at the catcher's sign or they can reveal the over-confidence of a rookie getting picked off at first. Haiku can also find meaningful moments in the stands or even in a passageway to the locker room where all we hear as a player leaves the last game of his career is the sound of his cleats echoing on the floor.

Fans of haiku will want this book for its outstanding haiku. Fans of baseball will want it for the way the haiku let them relive the joys and the sorrows of the game. The unforgettable images that pop up out of the pages of this collection capture the actions and atmospheres, the moods and tensions, the weathers and memories of America's national pastime—and Japan's.

Haiku often relate us to nature by invoking one of the four seasons, either by naming the season or by suggesting it. Baseball, too, is a game for all seasons. It is played in the spring, summer, and fall, and is enjoyed in retrospect during the winter. When participants and fans read about and discuss the game during the "off-season" they are in what is called "the hot stove league," from the days when people used to sit around a stove in the back of a country store or tavern to talk baseball. Baseball haiku follow that tradition, they help us to relive significant moments and aspects of the game. And they, too, can be enjoyed year-round.

In an essay on baseball haiku written for and read at a National Baseball Hall of Fame conference in 2001, Edward J. Rielly, one of the poets in this anthology, points out how fitting a topic baseball is for haiku:

> Baseball is an especially appropriate subject for haiku . . . Haiku usually seek some union of nature and humanity, and baseball grew out of a pastoral setting. The game still retains something of that natural setting, even in modern stadiums, but more so in minor league parks (the term "ballpark" itself recalls the game's origins) where the diamond is outdoors, the fans close to the field, the grass real, the dirt rises in small puffs as the runner slides into base, and trees and hills loom beyond the fences. So, among the major team sports, it is baseball that most clearly touches the natural world that is a vital dimension of haiku.

In Japanese haiku, to ensure nature is present in the poem it must contain what is called a season word or *kigo*. For traditionalists, this is a rule: if there is no kigo the poem is not a haiku. The kigo is a word that tells a reader in which season the moment evoked in the haiku is taking place. It can be the name of the season or it can be a word like "snow" to indicate winter, or "cherry blossoms" to indicate spring. The word *naitā* ("nah-ee-taahh," the Japanese adaptation of the coined English word "nighter," meaning "night game") indicates summer. It and the word "baseball" itself (either *yakyū* or *bēsubōru*), also suggesting summer, are the only kigo directly referring to the game that are listed in Japanese haiku almanacs or *saijiki*. (The word "baseball" is also listed as a seasonal topic or *kidai*.) That may be one reason so many Japanese baseball haiku seem to be about night games. The season words are arranged in such almanacs, along with haiku demonstrating their use, so that poets and readers alike can know which season custom and usage has dictated that a particular word will represent. Japanese poets have been using baseball as a subject for their haiku since 1890.

American haiku poets work in a less regimented fashion. They might imply, suggest, or actually name a season in their haiku, but they don't have to use a prescribed season word. They do have traditional indicators of seasons, however. A robin can suggest spring, a firecracker the Fourth of July, football autumn, and ice skates winter. Whether or not an American haiku poet always names or suggests a season in his haiku, nature will always be present, even if it is not immediately apparent. American poets in general take a freer approach to haiku than do their Japanese counterparts, just as American baseball players have a more relaxed, less rigid style of playing and training than most Japanese players.

Just as they do not have a kigo rule, the best writers of haiku in America rarely write in seventeen syllables. They write a free-verse haiku that usually has less. Trying to write haiku in seventeen syllables in English often results in using unnecessary words to fill out the count. Such words will destroy a haiku, which depends on concision and suggestibility for its effect. [The Japanese count syllables differently than we do—they count shorter elements, *onji,* as "syllables." The word "haiku," for example, is three *onji,* while we count it as two syllables. Ten to fourteen English syllables equal the time duration of seventeen Japanese onji.]

The passage of time in a baseball game also relates to haiku. Haiku is about the present moment: *now.* That is why almost all haiku are in the present tense. The present moment holds within it all time. For it is in all time, including past and future, where "now" occurs. The haiku moment expands into the infinite, for the reader is made one with all of nature through the particular aspect of nature to which the haiku relates him. This may be one reason R. H. Blyth (1898–1964), the most important translator of Japanese haiku into English, and others have asserted that "haiku is Zen." Time in baseball by its slow pace and open-endedness—there is no time limit as in other team sports—also makes it possible for us to experience those special moments during the game that are haiku moments. Again, Edward J. Rielly:

> The pace of baseball permits fans to view the game in distinct moments rather than as a blur of action or a complex fusion of bodies whose individual motions are almost impossible to decipher. Fans watch the individual fielder or batter, the baseball rising toward left field, the pitcher starting his windup, the graceful shortstop flying through the air to encircle a liner in his glove, the fleet runner stealing a base. Even when more than one player is involved, as in a double play, the viewer easily follows the movement from player to player, the experience so readily divisible into its component moments that the parts may even be immortalized (Tinker to Evers to Chance). These are moments that invite reflection and haiku.

And since haiku can present these moments in the present—in the now—no matter when they originally occurred, we can preserve moments from the past, either from games we have watched years earlier or from the memories of our own days on the diamonds of our youth. We can reexperience both the special and the most common elements of baseball as happening right now. For the lover of baseball, the common elements of the game are special, too—even something as simple as a long-ago game of catch.

Included along with the haiku in this book are poems in a related genre called *senryu*. Some poets even consider senryu a kind of haiku. They have the same form and both come out of the same tradition of Japanese linked verse (*renga*) and they are both concerned with an awareness of the world and the life around us. But where haiku relate us to nature, senryu make us more aware of human nature itself. For this reason, they are often humorous. American haiku poets write both haiku and senryu. Examples of senryu in this book are Alan Pizzarelli's "struck out — / back in the dugout / he kicks the water cooler" and Mike Dillon's "the last kid picked / running his fastest / to right field."

Pizzarelli, a major haiku poet, does a regular senryu section for the online magazine *simplyhaiku.com* and is himself one of America's leading senryu poets. One of his best-known senryu is "done / the shoeshine boy / snaps his rag." It is a senryu because it is about human nature—about how one can take pride in a work of perfection, whether it's a world-renowned symphony, a perfect curve, or a flawless shoeshine. There is, too, a touch of humor in the poem.

Until modern times in Japan haiku poets usually wrote only haiku, poems that followed the rules requiring seventeen syllables, a kigo, and a *kireji* (kireji are "cutting words" used for pauses or emphasis with no literal meaning, but possessing an emotional coloring); and senryu poets wrote only senryu, poems also requiring seventeen syllables, but not a kigo (though they may have them), nor kireji. For some time there have been signs that this division among Japanese poets is changing (Blyth noted the trend about fifty years ago), that is, some poets are writing both (though when a Japanese haiku poet writes a senryu, he will probably still call it a haiku). The eminent translator and scholar of Japanese poetry, Hiroaki Sato, recently described one way the distinction between the two has become blurred: the poem is often defined by who wrote it rather than what is in it because "if the author is known to write haiku, the pieces he or she writes are haiku; if the author is known to write senryu, the pieces she or he writes are senryu" (*Modern Haiku,* vol. 34.1, 2003). However, we have not included any Japanese baseball senryu in this book. Those we were able to find by senryu poets didn't seem to us to get to the spirit and essence of the game. They were more like journalistic comments or jokes, usually about players or teams in the news, or ephemeral topics that will be forgotten by next season.

The First Baseball Haiku

The story of baseball haiku begins with Masaoka Shiki (1867–1902), who was to become the fourth pillar in Japan's pantheon of great haiku masters (joining Bashō, Buson, and Issa). Shiki was only five years old and living on the island of Shikoku when baseball was being first taught to Japanese students in Tokyo by Horace Wilson. An American teacher at what is now Tokyo University, Wilson introduced the game there in 1872. It became very popular with both the students and faculty at the school. It soon spread to other schools and to amateur athletic clubs in the Tokyo area, and gradually from there to the rest of the country.

Shiki left his hometown of Matsuyama on Shikoku in 1883 and went to Tokyo to further his education. In 1884 he was accepted at Daigaku Yobimon (University Preparatory School). By this time baseball was already popular at the school. Shiki discovered the game there and immediately fell in love with it, so much so that his friends called him "baseball mad." He and a fellow classmate, Iwaoka, alternated with each other in playing pitcher and catcher for their school team. Catcher was Shiki's favorite position even though he threw left-handed, unusual for someone working behind the plate. It is said that he even practiced his catching technique in his room.

Shiki was so enthusiastic about baseball that when he went back to his hometown in the summer of 1889, he brought with him a ball and bat as a present for his friend Kawahigashi Hekigotō (1873–1937) and taught him the game. The next year, he also taught Takahama Kyoshi (1874–1959) how to play baseball. Hekigotō and Kyoshi would both become famous haiku poets, beginning as disciples of Shiki. After the master's early death in 1902, they became leaders of their own schools of haiku.

Shiki not only taught baseball to his friends, but is credited with having been the first to introduce it to his hometown of Matsuyama, and thus to the island of Shikoku. His writings on baseball later helped to popularize the game throughout Japan. The first baseball haiku we have by Shiki—by anyone—were written in 1890. He wrote four that year. Here is one of them: *spring breeze / this grassy field makes me / want to play catch.* We have a total of nine baseball haiku from his pen, or brush, and we've included them all in this book. Here is one he wrote in 1898:

natsukusa ya   bēsubōru no   hito tōshi

summer grass
baseball players far off
in the distance

In 1889, Shiki was diagnosed with tuberculosis and was
no longer able to play for the school team. The following
year, he went as a spectator to see the team play Meiji-gakuin
University (a Christian college). His friend Iwaoka was
pitching, but their school lost. Shiki recorded his disap-
pointment in his writings. He was the first Japanese writer
to use baseball as a literary subject. Besides composing
haiku, tanka, and fiction related to baseball, he also wrote
essays about it. In an article for the newspaper *Nippon,* in
1896, he described the game's rules and equipment, and
even translated baseball terms from English into Japanese.
Here is one of his tanka (lyric poems slightly longer than
haiku) written in 1898 (he wrote ten tanka on baseball, all
in 1898 or 1899):

hisakata no   Amerika bito no   hajime nishi
bēsubōru wa   mire do akanu kamo

under a faraway sky
the people of America
began baseball
I can watch it
forever

Tanka does not seem to be as adaptable to baseball as
haiku. Its lyric, romantic style leads the poet to generalize
about the subject, rather than to create details that can rep-

resent in vivid fashion the spirit of the game. The longer form—traditionally tanka has thirty-one syllables (onji) to the haiku's seventeen—seems to get in the way of the action. There is a tendency to go on rhapsodizing about the subject, which can result in banalities.

Even a great poet like Shiki could not capture the essence of the game in tanka the way he did in haiku. The one just quoted, while expressing an admirable sentiment, is simply a comment on the game and not a re-creation of any of its aspects. When he describes an aspect of the game in a tanka, it, too, is generalized and lacks any visual snap: *a high fly ball / having shot up to the clouds / drops back down again/ to wind up in the glove / of the waiting fielder.*

Shiki never lost his love for the sport. There still exists a photograph of him in his school baseball uniform. A large reproduction of the picture is prominently displayed in the Shiki-Kinen (Shiki Memorial) Haiku Museum in Matsuyama in a wall-size glass case along with copies of the haiku and tanka he wrote about baseball. For his contributions to baseball Shiki was elected to the Japanese Baseball Hall of Fame in 2002, the 144th to be chosen since the Hall of Fame was begun in 1959. Horace Wilson, the American credited with introducing baseball to Japan in 1872, is also in the Hall of Fame—elected in 2003.

Other Japanese Haiku Poets and Baseball

Following Shiki's personal output of nine baseball haiku, baseball as a subject in Japanese haiku seems to have been fairly rare until the advent of night games sometime in the 1930s or '40s and the subsequent development of the word *naitā* (nighter) as a season word for summer. And baseball haiku are still fairly uncommon.

After his death Shiki's disciples gradually parted from each other. Differing in their ideas about haiku and how to write them, they moved in different directions not only in the methods they used, but often in the subject matter they chose to write about. In Japanese haiku an acknowledged master usually becomes the head of a group, the members of which try to follow that master's ideas of what is the best way to write haiku. The leader is called *sensei* (literally "teacher," but often translated as "master"). When he dies, one of his pupils usually takes over as leader while others may leave to form their own groups. The two most important of Shiki's disciples were Kawahigashi Hekigoto and Takahama Kyoshi. As noted above, Shiki had not only been their haiku mentor but had also taught them the game of baseball. Hekigoto took over Shiki's job as editor of the haiku pages in the newspaper *Nippon,* thus becoming the most influential haiku poet and critic in the country. Kyoshi at first began to concentrate his energy on writing novels and essays, leaving the leadership of the haiku world to Hekigotō.

Shiki had revitalized haiku in Japan by introducing modern subjects and the use of a more contemporary language than the classical haiku allowed. Hekigotō opened up haiku to more experimentation than even Shiki had countenanced. He not only said haiku could use everyday language about any subject—new or old—but that they could be written in more or fewer than seventeen syllables. Traditionally the seventeen syllables are written in a single vertical line, but are in grammatical units of 5-7-5, which is why they are usually translated into three lines. Haiku has to be a short poem, but Hekigotō by writing some of his with more than twenty syllables was dangerously close to creating a "regular" free-verse poem. He did retain a fondness for the season word and felt a haiku should—at least usually—have one.

One of his followers, Ogiwara Seisensui (1884–1976), took the idea of a "free" haiku even further and advocated rejecting both the seventeen-syllable form and the season word. He also borrowed from Western poetics such modern techniques as symbolism, surrealism, and impressionism to widen haiku's horizons and give it new vitality. Following in his line of development were such barrier-breakers as Ozaki Hōsai (1885–1926), Taneda Santōka (1882–1940), and Nakatsuka Ippekirō (1887–1946) in the first half of the twentieth century; and Tohta Kaneko (b. 1919) and Natsuishi Ban'ya (b. 1955) in the last half and into the twenty-first century.

We might expect such poets to have written at least once about baseball in their haiku, but though we have one baseball haiku from Hekigotō we have found none from Seisensui or from any of the others. Both Santōka and Hōsai led monklike lives and their haiku are often about wandering in the mountains or living simply in a hut. However, Hōsai did write a haiku about the sport of sumo wrestling. Ippekirō, one of the most radical innovators, wrote a haiku about rugby, but none that we know of on baseball.

Tohta has written haiku about motorcycles, and such sports as boxing and soccer, but none on baseball that we could find. Natsuishi, though he writes about everything from Japanese mythology to boomerangs and atomic bombs, along with allusions to contemporary Western literature and a generous use of graphically explicit sexual imagery and symbolist obscurity, also seems not to have written directly about baseball. He does have one haiku about playing ball (*tama asobi*), which may refer to baseball, perhaps a game of catch. It opens with an image of a cloud in a wide sky forming the shape of a *manji* (swastika) and concludes: "so I play ball."

These poets who came after Seisensui took haiku into an avant-garde mode that has become a special haiku category in Japan: *gendai* (modern) haiku. The Gendai Haiku Association in Japan has over eight thousand members.

Alongside the strain of avant-garde haiku poets that branched out from Hekigotō, a more traditional line developed from Shiki's other major disciple, Kyoshi. Though he himself may have not brought the subject of baseball into his haiku (we have not found any), a number of haiku poets that were at first influenced by his more conservative poetics and later broke away from his group did write baseball haiku. After some years of concentrating his literary talents on trying to write novels, Kyoshi returned to making haiku his main focus in 1912 and immediately responded in a reactionary way to what Hekigotō and his followers were doing. Alarmed by the free rein these radicals were taking with the genre, he set out to try to return haiku to the traditional conventions he felt really defined haiku as haiku. He had taken over the editorship of Shiki's magazine *Hototogisu (Cuckoo)*, but had been using it mainly to publish prose. He now returned it to haiku. Using the time-honored image of "plum blossoms and bush warblers" as a symbol of all the conventions that went together to create the classical haiku, he began rallying a large following and soon his school of thought came to dominate haiku. It still dominates in spite of the very talented and vocal poets who are active outside the boundaries of this mainstream. Five-seven-five, kigo, and kireji are all thought to be essential characteristics of haiku by the vast majority of Japanese haiku poets.

Among the most important of the haiku poets temporarily taking their stand with Kyoshi and then opting for a more original kind of haiku was Mizuhara Shūōshi (1892–1981). He broke with Kyoshi's group (which was still gathered under the banner of *Hototogisu*) around 1930 to join with a group of younger poets associated with the magazine *Ashibi* (*Andromeda*). He wanted a more lyrical and imaginative haiku than he felt the traditionalists would allow. In 1935, he was joined by another deserter from the Kyoshi ranks, Yamaguchi Seishi (1901–1994), who wanted to include the things of the industrial age in his haiku such as trains, cars, guns, and elevators. He also wrote about a number of sports borrowed from the West, including rugby, golf, skating, and baseball. Shūōshi and Seishi lived in big cities and wrote about urban life, including big-league baseball games. Shūōshi is represented in this book by two night-game haiku plus a remarkable five-haiku sequence about an afternoon at the Meiji-Jingu Stadium, Tokyo's most traditional ballpark; and Seishi by five night-game haiku, one about a black ballplayer, probably one of the American ex-major leaguers who have played professional ball in Japan.

Also in line from Kyoshi is Akimoto Fujio (1901–1977), who was influenced by Seishi and joined that poet's group in 1948. A year later he formed his own group, Hyōkai (Frozen Sea). There is one baseball haiku of his included here, an unusual juxtaposition of a night game with a natural scene at a distant pond.

The rest of the Japanese poets represented in this book are an assortment of mavericks and traditionalists, some who to a large degree have found their own way in haiku after early influences and others who have started off with established masters and remained loyal to those roots. Yamazaki Hisao (b. 1927) studied under Kishi Fusanro, who had been a follower of Seishi. His haiku about a base-ball scorecard takes a very simple object with a complicated set of meanings and presents it vividly to reflect the excitement of the game. Takaha Shugyō (b. 1930) first wrote under the influence of Seishi and then studied with Akimoto Fujio. His haiku have an "intellectual lyricism," according to one critic. His evocation of the grass on a baseball diamond lets us feel it right under our feet. Arima Akito's (b. 1930) mentor was Yamaguchi Seison (1892–1988), who was in a line from Kyoshi. Arima has written only one baseball haiku. It evokes the coolness in the stands of a famous baseball stadium, Kōshien near Osaka. Hoshino Tsunehiko (b. 1935) has cotranslated Takaha into English and has worked in the International Department of the Museum of Haiku Literature in Tokyo for a number of years. His baseball haiku comes from observing his son learning to play the game.

Imai Sei (b. 1950) has nine baseball haiku in this book, which all demonstrate his ability to catch the telling details in any scene he is re-creating. He has been influenced by both Shiki's haiku technique of sketching from nature and the works of Western poets like Ezra Pound and the Imagists. The originality of his baseball haiku is perhaps partly due to his rarely depending on the kigo *naitā* (only two of them use it). Yotsuya Ryū (b. 1958) has been influenced by the free-style haiku of Ippekirō and by modern French poetry. We have two baseball haiku by Yotsuya: one about a game of catch on the beach and another that celebrates his baseball glove and green fields.

Taki Shun'ichi (1902–1996), a follower of Shūōshi who broke with him for a while to write *muki* (no season word) haiku, Ozawa Seiyūshi (1912–1945), who is considered a gendai poet, Kadokawa Genyoshi (1917–1975), who championed lyricism in haiku, and Suzuki Murio (1919–2004) were all original and innovative poets. Though each has only one or two baseball haiku in this anthology, they are extra-base hits worthy of the great games of baseball and haiku. Though we have probably missed many other baseball haiku written by Japanese poets, what we have found amounts to a literary treasure for baseball and haiku fans alike.

The First American Baseball Haiku

The first American baseball haiku was written by Jack Kerouac (1922–1969) more than a half century after Shiki's pioneering poems. In fact, Kerouac was one of the first American writers to write haiku on any subject. Though haiku were written about in English, and even translated, as early as the late nineteenth century, they had not been recognized as serious or important literature. One early translator even referred to haiku as "epigrams" and thought they were light verse of the most insignificant sort.

By the time of the Imagists in the second and third decades of the twentieth century, haiku had gained a bit more respect, but writers in English, possessing only inadequate translations, still misunderstood the genre. The Imagists did bring the ideals of concision and clarity into English-language poetry as a result of their partial knowledge of haiku, but the birth of real haiku in English had to wait until the second half of the century. Most early translators were in fact baffled by haiku's brevity and padded out their translations with too many words, trying to explain the haiku instead of just translating it. Some put them into seventeen syllables, which, as we have already noted, can cause problems. The evocativeness of the Japanese haiku was lost through the translators' wordiness.

It wasn't until after World War II, when the perceptive

and accurate translations of Harold G. Henderson (1889–1974) and R. H. Blyth were published, that American poets had the chance to understand haiku and were able to write their own. One of the first to do so was Gary Snyder, at the time a fledgling poet with an intense interest in the literatures of Japan and China, in Buddhism, and American Indian cultures. Snyder obtained all four volumes of Blyth's *Haiku,* published from 1949 to 1952. Jack Kerouac mentions seeing them in 1955 when he and Snyder first met. They were on a shelf in Snyder's shack in Berkeley. Snyder had probably obtained them shortly after their publication, for we know he was experimenting with haiku as early as 1952, when he wrote some in his journal while fire watching on Crater Mountain in the Cascades.

Besides introducing Kerouac to Blyth's books, Snyder helped teach him how to write haiku. In *The Dharma Bums* (1958) Kerouac reports that Snyder (called Japhy Ryder in the novel) told him, "A real haiku's gotta be as simple as porridge and yet make you see the real thing," and that he then quoted a haiku by Masaoka Shiki: "The sparrow hops / Along the verandah, / With wet feet." (It is a translation by Blyth.) "You see the wet footprints like a vision in your mind," added Snyder, "and yet in those few words you also see all the rain that's been falling that day and almost smell the wet pine needles."

After Kerouac learned about haiku he continued to write and experiment with them until his death fourteen years later. Notes for his haiku were often first jotted down in the small notebooks he carried in the pocket of his checkered lumberjack shirt. He had already been using them to make quick sketches in prose for his novels.

Snyder used *his* knowledge of haiku to write a different kind of poetry and he has become one of America's most important writers on nature and the environment. The other Beat writers either did not attempt haiku or were not very good at it. At various times, Allen Ginsberg tried his hand at haiku, even publishing a small chapbook of them, but they are mostly unexceptional. He wrote none on baseball. Nor, as far as we know, has Snyder ever written any.

Kerouac had practically no contact with the American haiku movement and only a few of his haiku saw print during his lifetime. He wrote what is probably the first American baseball haiku sometime around 1958. It first "appeared" on a recording, *Blues and Haikus,* in 1959. Kerouac read more than thirty of his haiku on this recording, with Zoot Sims and Al Cohn taking turns playing short jazz comments on the saxophone after each one. The haiku were not printed in the notes with the album. This is the haiku:

Empty baseball field
— A robin,
Hops along the bench

Though this haiku does not directly present aspects of the game itself, Kerouac manages to evoke a combination of emotional feelings that we can associate with the game. First there is the lonely feeling called up by the emptiness of the field, then the contrasting sense of promise provided by the entrance of the robin—a sign of spring indicating that ballplayers will also soon appear on the field. Kerouac brought baseball into his haiku, because he wanted to make *American* haiku. As far as we know, he never knew of Shiki's baseball haiku, nor any other baseball haiku. Blyth does not include any in his books. Translations of Shiki's baseball haiku did not appear in English until many years later. Janine Beichman in her book *Masaoka Shiki*, published in

1982, translates one of Shiki's baseball tanka, but does not mention his baseball haiku. The first record we've been able to find of an English translation of a Shiki baseball haiku is in a book published by the Matsuyama Shiki-Kinen Museum in 1986, *Shiki and Matsuyama*. [See the Book List.] Kerouac wrote only one other baseball haiku, which we also include in this book.

Jack Kerouac was a baseball player for both his high school and prep school teams. He played in the outfield and threw and batted right-handed. Where he really excelled, however, was in football. He was a star on the gridiron in high school and at the Horace Mann School for Boys, a preparatory school in New York City where Columbia University sent him for a year (1939–40). He entered the university on a football scholarship in the fall of 1940, but injuries plagued him and the promise of a great college football career was never realized.

He wrote one football haiku. It too relates to the loneliness of an empty playing field. It has the feeling of *sabi,* the bittersweet sadness of being alone in time, an element valued in haiku by the Japanese masters. The season is, of course, autumn:

Crossing the football field,
    coming home from work,
The lonely businessman

Other American Haiku Poets and Baseball

In American haiku there is no system of masters and disciples such as exists in Japanese haiku. For the pioneers of American haiku, and those who have followed, the main teachers have been the great translators of Japanese haiku.

A number of American poets found Blyth's books around the same time as Kerouac or shortly afterward. Cor van den Heuvel discovered haiku—and Blyth's books—after hearing Gary Snyder talk about short poems at a poets' gathering in San Francisco in 1958.

The first haiku magazine to be published in English, *American Haiku,* was started in Wisconsin in 1963 and the Haiku Society of America began in New York City in 1968. The Haiku Society was one of the first groups to study and write haiku in the United States and it was started by Harold G. Henderson and Leroy Kanterman, the editor of one of the earliest English-language haiku magazines, *Haiku West.* Cor van den Heuvel and Alan Pizzarelli first met at one of the Society's meetings in the early 1970s.

The Haiku Society later helped to spawn groups all over the United States and Canada. There are now regional divisions and smaller haiku-workshop groups within the Society, but there are many independent groups as well. Many of the poets in this book belong to such groups. Cor van den Heuvel, Bruce Kennedy, and Brenda Gannam belong to the Spring Street Haiku Group, which meets at Poets House in New York City. Gannam, whose senryu rival our best stand-up comics, is its coordinator. Jim Kacian has been involved with the Towpath Haiku Group, in the Washington, D.C., area, while at the same time being an influential figure in international haiku as poet, editor, publisher, and proselytizer. His haiku about a catcher's returning the ball to the mound after an inning-ending strike lights up one of the pages further on in this book. John Stevenson and Tom Clausen belong to a very small haiku group, four or five poets, in upstate New York called the Dim Sum Haiku Group. They meet in a Chinese restaurant. Michael Dylan Welch was once active with the Haiku Poets of

Northern California. Now in the Seattle area, he is involved with the Northwest Regional Group of the HSA. Raffael de Gruttola helped found the Boston Haiku Society in 1987. He has also served as president of the HSA, as have several other poets represented in this anthology. Some of his baseball haiku come from watching Red Sox games.

These groups are not headed by masters or sensei. Though the larger groups have officers for administrative purposes, the smaller groups, where the writing and critical work goes on, usually have only members, one of whom will be simply a "coordinator." That person will arrange for a meeting place and may moderate the meetings. Though some major haiku poets are known to have influenced other poets, they have rarely been considered "masters" in the traditional Japanese sense. Many Midwest haiku poets were influenced by the innovative haiku poet Father Raymond Roseliep (1917–1983), who taught at Loras College in Dubuque, Iowa. He seems not to have written about baseball, but Lee Gurga, Randy Brooks, and Edward J. Rielly who have, and are in this book, all looked to Roseliep at one time or another for inspiration. Haiku poets also help each other with their creative efforts by conferring by e-mail or regular mail as well as through group meetings.

Arizona Zipper was one of the first poets after Kerouac to put baseball in haiku. His "Hopping over the mound" was written in 1981. Another early bird with baseball haiku was Alan Pizzarelli, who published a folded broadside in 1988 called *Baseball Poems*. It was a sequence of nine haiku and senryu about the game. Since then, a large number of American haiku poets have tried to capture baseball moments in their haiku and senryu. Bud Goodrich, who has published many fine senryu on the game, wrote one as early as 1992. His "Squeeze play" first appeared in the *Midwest*

Haiku Anthology that year. Cor van den Heuvel, though he had been writing haiku as early as 1959, didn't publish any baseball haiku until 1993, when several of them appeared in the *haibun* (prose with haiku) "A Boy's Seasons" in *Modern Haiku.*

One of the most prolific and perceptive creators of American baseball haiku is Ed Markowski, who has twenty-one base hits in this book. He started writing haiku in 1989, but didn't publish any of them until 2001. His haiku about box scores, the hot-stove league, and dingers bring aspects of the game before us more vividly in just a few words than do many of the celebrated essays of famed sportswriters.

Michael Ketchek writes tellingly about what it can feel like to strike out, and even gives us a nostalgic moment from a game of Wiffle Ball in a long-ago driveway. Dan McCullough didn't start writing haiku until the year 2000. His baseball haiku, however, are worthy of a veteran. From the field where his closer shakes his head in the rain to a barroom where the game takes on a new perspective, McCullough captures moments of the national pastime that awaken the imagination.

Also relative rookies in the haiku game, Mathew V. Spano (his first published haiku was in 1996) and Chad Lee Robinson (first published haiku 2003) have already demonstrated more than just promise on the haiku diamond. Spano knows how to relate nature to the game and to the poetic form with his chill wind in the bleachers and with the lonely night of his home run ball. While Robinson has only one haiku here, it's a hit that shines through the words and the night like the game of baseball shines in the hearts of its fans.

All the American poets in these pages, rookies and veterans, are exceptional. We have included one Canadian star as well, George Swede. Keeping in mind how Canadian players and even Canadian ball clubs have contributed to the glory of the U.S. major leagues, we count ourselves lucky to have a great pitcher of haiku like George decorating our roster.

As with the Japanese haiku poets, we may have missed some good baseball haiku by American and Canadian haiku poets, but here is a representative selection by some of the top players in the game, both in Japan and North America.

—Cor van den Heuvel
Spring 2006

AMERICAN

BASEBALL HAIKU AND SENRYU

Bud Goodrich 1919

Arthur "Bud" Goodrich still remembers being taken out of his first-grade class along with his twin brother Charles ("Chuck") by their father to go to a Yankees-White Sox game at Comiskey Park hoping to see the great Babe Ruth hit a home run. However, the Sultan of Swat struck out four times, and the boys had to wait for a future game to see him get a hit. In retrospect, as lifelong White Sox fans the brothers shouldn't feel too bad—hopefully the Babe's performance allowed a Sox win. (Their real love, though, is for the Cubs.)

Bud learned about haiku in the 1970s from an article in *The Writer* that mentioned *Modern Haiku* magazine. After a year or two Bud's haiku and senryu began to be accepted by *MH* editor Robert Spiess. In 1992 his first baseball haiku, "Squeeze play," appeared in *The Midwest Haiku Anthology* (High/Coo Press). It is actually a senryu and all of his poems in this selection are senryu. His chapbook *Rhubarb! The Collected Senryu and Haiku of Bud Goodrich* was published in 2003 by Deep North Press.

Born December 20, 1919 in Winnetka, Illinois, Goodrich has lived there all his life, except for prep school, Oberlin College, and four years in the U.S. Army during World War II. In the 1930s he attended the Asheville School in Asheville, North Carolina, where he played first base for the school team. The coach proclaimed him the "First Baseman of the Decade." He throws and bats right-handed.

Just when the rhubarb begins
— TV commercial

Manager, umpire
shadow-boxing
jaw to jaw

Intentional walk —
each fan winding up
his own boo

World Series replay —
the boy squeezes an umpire's
home run call

Rookie's first hit —
picked off at first

Squeeze play
the umpire whisk brooming
home plate

Home run trot —
the batter's eye a tape
measuring the distance

Jack Kerouac 1922–1969

The king of the Beats, Jack Kerouac chronicled the bohemian lifestyle that came to characterize a generation. *On the Road* captured the wide sweep of the American landscape and the intense tempo of modern times—cars speeding down highways, the cities' neon glitter, and the swinging sounds of jazz. His books also record periods of quiet introspection and communing with nature. Kerouac learned about haiku from Gary Snyder in 1955 while in the San Francisco Bay area. In *The Dharma Bums* (1958), Kerouac mentions that Snyder had R. H. Blyth's four-volume *Haiku* in his shack in Berkeley and tells how they talked about ways to write haiku. Of the Beat writers, Kerouac was the most perfectly attuned to haiku and was soon writing good ones. He wrote the first American baseball haiku ("Empty baseball field"). It came out in 1959 on *Blues and Haikus,* a record on which he read his haiku with jazz accompaniment. He wrote only one other.

Born in Lowell, Massachusetts, March 12, 1922, Kerouac became a star athlete at Lowell High, winning a football scholarship to Columbia University. Though best known as a football player—at Horace Mann prep school and Columbia—Kerouac played in the outfield for the Horace Mann baseball team in 1940. He threw and batted right-handed.

> How cold! — late
>   September baseball —
> the crickets

Empty baseball field
— A robin,
Hops along the bench

Helen Shaffer 1923

Born August 18, 1923, in Chambersburg, Pennsylvania, Helen Shaffer (pronounced Shay-fer) grew up there and still lives in the same house she lived in as a child. Though she didn't play much baseball herself, her mother (more than her father) was interested in the sport and took her to major league games. For a long time their favorite team was the Brooklyn Dodgers.

Later, Helen became a fan of the Pittsburgh Pirates and liked to go to see them play in Three Rivers Stadium (since torn down), which she says was the most beautiful ballpark she has ever seen. She has also followed the Philadelphia Athletics, when Connie Mack was the manager, and the Philadelphia Phillies.

A writer all her life, she has written and published lots of light verse. It has appeared on greeting cards, in *The Philadelphia Sunday Bulletin,* and in *The Wall Street Journal.* She writes that "A discarded library copy of *The Tale of Genji,* which I bought for fifteen cents sparked an interest in Japanese poetry." In the late 1980s she started writing haiku and soon joined the Haiku Society of America. Her haiku and tanka have been published in a number of journals. Among her favorite poets are Yamaguchi Seishi and Nick Virgilio.

She wrote her first baseball haiku in 1998 when she heard Red Moon Press was doing an anthology of baseball haiku (*Past Time,* 1999). Her "drooping flag," accepted for the book, shows one way nature is closely involved with the game: it can signal to a manager how to position his defensive players.

drooping flag . . .
the visitors' manager
moves a fielder

Cor van den Heuvel 1931

This poet was born on March 6, 1931, in Biddeford, Maine, and grew up in Maine and New Hampshire. He discovered haiku in San Francisco in 1958 when he overheard Gary Snyder talking about short poems at a Sunday gathering of the Robert Duncan/Jack Spicer poetry group in North Beach. Back in Maine the following spring, he began writing haiku himself and began reading them at the Cafe Zen, a Beat-style coffee house in Ogunquit. In the fall, he moved to Boston to become the house poet at the Salamander Cafe. The summer of 1960 he worked on a fishing trawler out of Provincetown during the day and read his haiku in a bar at night. He then went to New York where he was involved with the poetry readings at the Tenth Street Coffee House. He self-published his first chapbook of haiku in 1961. *The Haiku Anthology*, which he has edited through three editions, first appeared in 1974. A selection of his baseball haiku, *Play Ball,* was published in 1999 by Red Moon Press. In Matsuyama in 2002, he was awarded the Masaoka Shiki International Haiku Prize. (The award included a medal decorated with a baseball and crossed baseball bats.) Van den Heuvel was known as "Dutchy" when he played catcher in the late 1940s for the Comets, a sandlot team in Dover, New Hampshire. He throws and bats right-handed.

> first warm day
> fitting my fingers into the mitt
> pounding the pocket

lingering snow
the game of catch continues
into evening

a spring breeze
flutters the notice
for baseball tryouts

geese flying north
the pitcher stops his windup
to watch

through the blue sky
the tape-wrapped baseball trails
a black streamer

baseball cards
spread out on the bed
April rain

downpour
windswept spray blows across
the outfield

biking to the field
under a cloudless sky
my glove on the handlebars

under the lights
hitting it out of the park
and into the night

dispute at second base
the catcher lets some dirt
run through his fingers

the batter checks
the placement of his feet
"Strike One!"

the ball sky-high
as the crack of the bat
reaches the outfield

after the grand slam
the umpire busy
with his whisk broom

conference on the mound
the pitcher looks down
at the ball in his hand

summer afternoon
the long fly ball to center field
takes its time

changing pitchers
the runner on first looks up
at a passing cloud

long day
the right fielder is playing
with a dog

light rain
a line drive knocks up dust
between second and third

the infield chatter
floats out to deep center
summer breeze

in the outfield's
late-afternoon shadows
the coolness of my glove

perfect game, end of seven
in the dugout the pitcher
sits alone

hot day
listening to the ball game
while washing the car

Ted hits another homer
a seagull high over right field
gets out of the way

9th inning
moths fly around
the ballpark lights

stolen base
the bench does its own
wave

the catcher cocks his arm
halfway to third, the runner
— hesitates

pitcher and catcher
head for the dugout
the batter stares at his bat

after the game
a full moon rises over
the left field fence

cold day
the traded catcher's
empty locker

autumn leaves
scatter across the infield
the pitcher blows on his fingers

a baseball
in the tied catcher's mitt
snow deepens

March thaw
the sounds of a game of catch
from the driveway

AT THE BALLPARK

early morning
cool shadows in the stands
of the small ballfield

spring training
an old timer plays pepper
with three rookies

college ballpark
fungoes one after another
into the blue sky

autumn dusk
an empty baseball field
in the rain

Raffael de Gruttola 1935

Born on May 15, 1935, in Cambridge, Massachusetts, Raffael de Gruttola grew up in Somerville, where he lived next to a baseball park. He played a lot of baseball as a boy, becoming the starting shortstop for an outstanding Somerville High School team that lost the State Championship Game to Springfield in Fenway Park, home of the Red Sox. He throws and bats right-handed. A Red Sox fan, he saw many Sox games when young by knowing how to sneak into Fenway. He remembers getting autographs from Ted Williams and other Boston greats. He went to Boston and Northeastern Universities after serving in the U.S. Army.

His first interest in poetry was free verse, but he started writing haiku in the sixties after reading Kenneth Yasuda and R. H. Blyth. In 1984 he self-published *Where ashes float,* a collection of free-verse poems with a selection of haiku at the end. His first haiku in a magazine was in Hal Roth's *Wind Chimes.* In 1987 he helped start the Boston Haiku Society and has served as its president. He has also been president of the Haiku Society of America. In recent years his work in *haiga* has received particular notice. Collaborating with several artists, he writes haiku as integral parts of their limited-edition prints.

> the umpire signals
> time-out
> a beach ball in the outfield

lost in the lights
the high fly ball that
never comes down

the umpire with raised arms!
a trail of dust still circling
the infield

puddles
in the batter's box
abandoned sandlot

Sylvia Forges-Ryan 1937

Sylvia Forges-Ryan writes, "My interest in baseball began in the fifth grade, when my classmate, Jack Nicholson, the actor, and I were taken to a Yankee doubleheader as a reward for being the top spellers in our class. Though I longed after that at many a recess to hit the ball over our schoolyard fence and score a home run, it never happened and I mostly had to content myself with watching others play, spending many summer evenings at local sandlot games." Sylvia throws and bats right-handed. Long a fan of the New York Yankees, she once had a crush on Whitey Ford.

Born in New York City April 6, 1937, she grew up on the New Jersey Shore, in a town called Neptune City. She received both a BA and an MA in English Literature from Bucknell, and an MA in Liberal Studies, with an emphasis on writing and poetry, from Wesleyan.

In 1983, now living in Connecticut, she took an adult education class in haiku and wrote her first haiku. She soon began publishing in the haiku magazines. From 1991 through 1993 she was the editor of the Haiku Society of America's *Frogpond*. Her haiku have won a number of awards, including the HSA's Harold Henderson Award and The British Haiku Society's R. H. Blyth Award. In 2003 she was invited to speak on haiku at the World Haiku Festival in The Netherlands. She has given haiku workshops in various venues, including The Insight Meditation Society and Harvard University. In 2002 she coauthored *Take a Deep Breath: The Haiku Way to Inner Peace,* published by Kodansha International and reprinted in Russia by Sophia Press.

waiting to bat
the hitter swats
a swarm of gnats

sandlot players
a mockingbird sings
the umpire's call

rained out
the coos of pigeons echo
in the empty stadium

Arizona Zipper 1940?

This rara avis from the White Mountains was born, with a different name, circa 1940 in North Conway, New Hampshire, and grew up in nearby Fryeburg, Maine, in a large rambling farmhouse opposite Fryeburg Academy. He was given a baseball glove at the age of seven and was often seen playing shortstop or second base in pick-up games in one of the ballfields across the street. When he entered the academy he made the team, but quit because the coach kept him on the bench. He played basketball and ran cross-country.

In Cambridge, Massachusetts, after a year at Emerson College, he worked in a tobacco shop (he is a longtime pipe smoker) and took up painting. He was next sighted in Kentucky apprenticed to a sculptor, who sent him to England to study with Henry Moore. His involvement with a girl quickly ended that and he returned to the States. It may have been about this time that he legally became Arizona Zipper. He then went to Alaska as a doghandler for a woman dog-sled racer. He entered the University of Alaska in 1968 to study art and found haiku in a book on Issa in the university library. He later surfaced in New York City where in the late '70s he discovered the Haiku Society of America.

Among his art-related activities since moving back to Fryeburg in the '80s are: fulfilling a vow of silence for a year, creating four hand-printed books with drawings in limited editions (five copies each), and writing an acclaimed series of haiku about fairs. He wrote his first baseball haiku, "Hopping over the mound," in 1981. A lifelong Red Sox fan, he throws and bats right-handed.

Hopping over the mound
and into the dugout —
the first robin.

A harvest moon
    every eye turned
        to a running bunt.

Bottom of the ninth
　　in the dugout
　　　　a row of bent heads.

George Swede 1940

One of the world's most accomplished haiku and senryu poets, George Swede was born in Riga, Latvia, on November 20, 1940, and from the age of seven grew up in British Columbia, Canada: first in Oyama, Okanagan Valley, and then from age ten in Vancouver. He played sandlot ball during his teen years and liked to play first base. He throws and bats right-handed. Swede attended the University of British Columbia (BA in psychology), Dalhousie University (MA), and studied at Indiana University. He's lived in Toronto since 1967, where he has had a long career at Ryerson Polytechnic University. He is currently the Chair of the Department of Psychology and the School of Justice Studies.

Just as Canada has teams in U.S. baseball leagues, most notably the Toronto Blue Jays in the American League, and Canadians play for American baseball teams, George is on our roster of American Baseball Haiku Poets. George was a Blue Jays season ticketholder for about five years during the time the team won its *two* World Series, 1992 and 1993. He first learned about haiku in 1968 during a creative writing class at the Three Schools of Art in Toronto and even wrote a few, but he didn't became seriously interested in writing haiku until 1976 when he was asked to review Makoto Ueda's *Modern Japanese Haiku: An Anthology*. He published his first haiku in *Bonsai* in 1977. The same year, with Eric Amann and Betty Drevniok, he cofounded the Haiku Society of Canada. He has published many books of haiku and other poetry. His latest haiku book is *Almost Unseen* from Brooks Books.

empty baseball field
a dandelion seed floats through
the strike zone

village ball game
through knotholes in the old fence
evening sunbeams

crack of the bat
the outfielder circles under
the full moon

Bill Pauly 1942

Born in Davenport, Iowa, on April 20, 1942, Bill Pauly moved with his family at the age of five to Dubuque, where he presently lives. He has lived most of his life in the Midwest and writes that he had a happy childhood, able to play outdoors a lot, wandering alone or with his three brothers through meadows and along meandering creeks. His mother was an amateur gymnast while his father played (and umpired) baseball and softball. Both were skilled bowlers.

Bill played baseball from an early age. "We played countless sandlot pick-up games," he reports, "at Dubuque's Comiskey Park, and [various] playgrounds. I also played three years of high school baseball, three summers of Holy Name League ball, three years at Loras College in Dubuque (Division 3, wooden bats, batting average about .333), and a few summers of Prairie League Semi-Pro ball." He usually played first base, batting and throwing right-handed. Bill's family has always been Cardinals' fans. Some of his heroes were Stan Musial, Enos Slaughter, and Dizzy Dean.

He's been writing haiku since the early 1960s, when he had the good fortune of taking a creative writing class at Loras taught by Raymond Roseliep. At that time Roseliep, already an important poet, was making his own first attempts at writing haiku. Bill's relationship with Roseliep grew into a mentoring one and then a friendship that lasted until Roseliep's death in 1983. Pauly has been teaching English and writing for about thirty years, mainly at Loras, where he even taught a course in haiku writing.

country field —
home run rolling
past the headstones

pop foul
ripping through the maple . . .
whirligigs

the ballplayers
running into dragonflies
marsh grass in left field

taking the field
the home team breathes halos
into moonlight

season over
the outfield ivy
red again

Edward J. Rielly 1943

Born December 22, 1943, in Darlington, Wisconsin, Edward J. Rielly grew up on a farm where he spent many hours playing baseball against an old red barn. He played softball during recess at his one-room country school, collected thousands of baseball cards (which he still has), and was on his high school baseball team. His favorite team was (and still is) the Chicago White Sox, and his all-time favorite player is Nellie Fox. He still remembers his father coming in from milking and sitting down beside the radio to listen to the White Sox or Milwaukee Braves games until he would doze off, usually around the seventh inning.

Rielly got his BA at Loras College in Dubuque, Iowa, and his MA and PhD from Notre Dame. He moved to Maine in 1978. He now chairs the English Department at Saint Joseph's College of Maine, from which he recently received a faculty fellowship. He has published two books on baseball and American culture, is doing a related book on football, and has written a biography of F. Scott Fitzgerald. He has published many baseball haiku and other baseball poems. His "entry into haiku" was a result of his reading the haiku of his creative-writing professor at Loras, Father Raymond Roseliep, one of America's early haiku masters.

Rielly has lectured at the National Baseball Hall of Fame on the relationship between baseball and haiku. His paper "Baseball Haiku: Bashō, the Babe, and the Great Japanese-American Trade," is a seminal essay in English on the subject. Among his nine chapbooks of poetry are five collections of haiku.

the boy not chosen
steps over home plate,
picks up his books

spring melt . . .
a baseball rises
beneath the forsythia

home run drive
into the cornfield —
fielder and girlfriend disappear

autumn wind
   rain blowing into
      the young catcher's face mask

April shower
the obituary leads me
to an old baseball card

Michael Fessler 1944

Born in Topeka, Kansas, on December 1, 1944, Michael Fessler grew up in northern Kentucky, where he played Little League Baseball from the age of six. He was on his high school team at Covington Catholic High School, playing shortstop and pitcher. He throws right, but is a switch-hitter. He was a fan of the Cincinnati Reds who played just across the Ohio River. He writes: "My favorite player on the Reds was Ted Kluszewski: My uncle knew Big Klu and took me to meet him after one of the Reds' games. Big Klu's trademark was sleeveless jerseys. He had industrial-strength muscles and brown bags under his eyes. Sad eyes. I also liked Gus Bell who played center. I went over to Crosley Field quite a few times with my dad and uncle, but I usually watched the games on TV or listened to them on radio with my grandfather." Fessler attended The Catholic University of America in Washington, D.C., on an athletic scholarship to play basketball.

In 1986, after seven years in San Francisco, an interest in Japanese culture led to his moving to Japan. He now teaches English at Waco University in Tokyo and catches the Japan Series each year on TV. He also watches U.S. baseball when it is on (which is when Ichiro, Matsui, or Iguchi are playing).

Though Fessler knew about haiku in college (from reading about Pound's "In a Station of the Metro"), he didn't start writing his own until after he went to Japan. His first published haiku appeared in the *Mainichi Daily News* in 1986. His haiku collection *The Sweet Potato Sutra* was published by Bottle Rockets Press in 2004.

August heat
umpire and manager
nose to nose

dust storm trick:
infielders
face the outfield

diving catch
some dandelion puffs
in center field

change of pitchers
the right fielder puts his glove
over his face

bottom of the ninth
the rookie stares
at his clean spikes

David Elliott 1944

David Elliott's interest in haiku began in college when he came across the Peter Pauper Press haiku anthologies. But it was not until he got inspired by Gary Snyder's poetry while doing graduate work in English at Syracuse that he began to take haiku more seriously. Aided by his future wife's enthusiasm for Asian culture ("it was she who put R. H. Blyth's anthologies into my hands in the late 1960s") he began to be more critically aware of haiku's importance and to make attempts at writing them. It was his discovery of the North American haiku community in the late '70s, however, that turned him into a haiku poet. He teaches English at Keystone College in Pennsylvania, is an "avid jazz fan and a very amateur jazz saxophonist," and likes to go mountain climbing in the Adirondacks.

Elliott was born in Minneapolis on December 26, 1944. He writes that "Baseball has always been my favorite sport and while growing up I was a fan of the Minneapolis Millers, a triple-A farm team for the New York Giants. Once a year the Giants came to town for an exhibition game, and one of the highlights of my childhood was watching Willie Mays hitting home runs. My favorite big league team, though, was the Dodgers. I was never on a school team but played a lot of neighborhood ball. My favorite position was first base. As a kid I loved my special first-baseman's mitt (a "Big Klu," endorsed by Ted Kluszewski) and lived for those one-handed catches stretched out with my foot on the base. My baseball haiku, however, come mostly from watching my sons play little league ball."

Shielding his eyes
with his baseball glove . . .
    first geese

Empty bleachers —
on the freshly raked baseline
pigeon tracks

Two herons
slowly fly over
the little league field

Flash of lightning —
all the little leaguers
look up

Night game
a softball soars
through swarms of gnats

Gerard John Conforti 1948

Best known for his tanka, Gerard John Conforti is also a fine haiku poet. The title of his selected haiku, *Pale Moonlight* (1999), suggests the romantic, lyric sensibility that makes him such a good tanka poet. It also tends to tinge much of his poetry with a Poe-like melancholy, as in his haiku sequence "From the Mental Ward." Conforti started writing haiku in 1978 and wrote his first tanka in 1986, learning about the latter from William J. Higginson's *The Haiku Handbook*.

The sensibility he brings to his poetry was hard won. Conforti was born in New York City on February 26, 1948. When he was four years old, his mother had a major breakdown and was confined to Rockland State Hospital. Gerard and his brothers were put into the Mount Loretto Orphanage on Staten Island, where he would stay until he was nineteen. Though unhappy at the orphanage, he found comfort in the woods and fields surrounding it. His love for nature would later attract him to poetry. He also enjoyed sports and played in the outfield for the Mount Loretto baseball team.

When Gerard left the orphanage he went into the armed services, but was discharged as not suitable. He has had mental problems over the years and attempted suicide at least twice. After being homeless on the streets of New York City, he was helped by his brother to get a job and a room in a rooming house on Staten Island. There he began to write poetry. In 1971 he entered Staten Island Community College and later graduated from Richmond College with a BA in English. He continues to live on Staten Island.

with a full count
the batter misses a hard fastball
dust from the catcher's glove

rain delay
the fans put up umbrellas
of different colors

as he winds up
the pitcher's long shadow
covers first base

night game
the glare of the lights
on the outfielders' glasses

a blimp
above the baseball stadium
floats by the moon

John Stevenson 1948

Born October 9, 1948, in Ithaca, New York, John Stevenson was raised in rural areas around that city—in the Finger Lakes region. He played pick-up baseball in the fields and yards around his home, and participated in little league through elementary school and junior high. He usually played catcher or second base.

"My first glove," he writes, "was probably an antique when I got it—very primitive. My first *new* glove was a Christmas present when I was eight. My favorite teams were the Yankees and the Dodgers—before they deserted Brooklyn. I remember seeing my first televised baseball game and being deeply impressed that I could see Mickey Mantle batting 'right now' and 'close up.' All the time I was interested in baseball, I was also interested in art, writing, and theater. These interests gradually supplanted most of my athletic interests during high school. I went to college as an art major and finished with a degree in theater.

"I heard my first haiku from a Japanese actress (in July 1992). She recited it in Japanese and then gave me an English translation. It was Bashō's poem about the crow settling on a bare branch. Within a month of that encounter, I was writing and publishing haiku."

Stevenson was a professional actor for most of his twenties and has been long involved with a kind of improvisational theater called Playback Theatre. He became a member of the Haiku Society of America in 1993 and was its president in 2000. He's been the editor of the society's magazine, *Frogpond,* since 2005. Red Moon Press has published two collections of his haiku.

extra innings
a runner's shadow
down the third base line

Lee Gurga 1949

Lee Gurga grew up in Chicago, where he was born on July 28, 1949. He attended the University of Illinois Urbana-Champaign. As a boy he lived half a block from a park where he got to play ball pretty much every day during the summer. He covered first base most of the time, but played in the outfield for a game called "pitcher's hands out." He throws lefty and bats right.

His favorite major league team? "The one and only Chicago White Sox. I lived on the north side, so you might think I would be a Cubs fan, but my grandfather, who was originally a Southsider, used to take me to Comiskey Park, where I grew up watching Nellie Fox, Louis Aparicio, and Minny Minoso. My grandmother could make him move to the north side, but she couldn't make him a Cubs fan!" When the Sox swept the Astros in the 2005 World Series, Lee, who had been at the first game, was, needless to say, jubilant.

The poet's first exposure to haiku was in a book of translations by R. H. Blyth he found in a bookstore when he was in high school. He was soon writing his own. His haiku are heavily rooted in the Midwest, often evoking its vast landscapes and endless skies. Gurga is a past president of The Haiku Society of America (1997) and was the editor of *Modern Haiku* from 2002 to 2006. He writes a regular haiku column for the *Solares Hill Newspaper* in Key West, where he vacations. Recent books include: *Fresh Scent* (Brooks Books, 1998), *Haiku, A Poet's Guide* (Modern Haiku Press, 2003), and *Autumn Mosquito* (Modern Haiku Press, 2005).

Louisville Slugger
the boy's fingertips caress
the trademark

the pitching coach
strides slowly to the mound —
dust devils

pitching change
a butterfly follows a wave
through the upper deck

hangovers in suits
climb onto the team bus
summer morning

rumble of thunder
the boy still looking for the ball
in the tall grass

David Giacalone 1949

Born in Rochester, New York, on December 9, 1949, David Giacalone lived there until going to Georgetown University, School of Foreign Service (BSFS 1971), and Harvard Law School. After about twenty years in Washington, he moved to Schenectady, New York. A former lawyer and divorce mediator, he enjoys "playing bocce with friends; listening to mystery novels, and being the editor-proprietor (along with several alter egos) of the *f/k/a* Weblog, which features 'one-breath poetry and breathless punditry,' and has an audience primarily comprised of legal professionals and extra-legal haijin."

In grammar school, Giacalone played three years of Midget League (softball), then two years of little league, playing second base and pitching. In the 1980s, he occasionally played on office softball teams. He throws and bats right-handed. About haiku, he writes: "First learned of (real) haiku circa 1998, when, due to a chronic illness, I said to myself, 'I'd like to do something literary, but I've only got enough attention span and energy for haiku.' I wrote only a couple haiku a year until I started writing in earnest in 2004, when I decided to write one a day and began posting them at my Weblog as part of my mission to be a Haiku Advocate. My haiku have since appeared in various haiku journals and in the *Legal Studies Forum*."

squinting to see him
another generation
sent to right field

law office picnic
the ump consults
his Blackberry

Alan Pizzarelli 1950

Alan Pizzarelli was born January 12, 1950, of an Italian-American family in Newark, New Jersey. Raised in the first ward's Little Italy, he showed an early interest in music. By age fourteen he had his own band and performed as lead singer, bass guitarist, and song writer. In the late '60s while working at the *Newark Star Ledger*, he became friends with the poet Louis Ginsberg (Allen Ginsberg's father). Amused by the punning verse Louis wrote for the paper, Alan began writing one-line humorous observations on the human condition he later learned were senryu. He was also writing short poems that a friend told him were haiku. In 1970 his haiku and senryu were accepted by *Haiku* magazine. He then started attending meetings of The Haiku Society of America in New York City and met Harold G. Henderson, who taught him the finer distinguishing characteristics of haiku and senryu. Pizzarelli's own senryu and critical writings have helped to define the genre in English. His first book of haiku and senryu was *Karma Pomes* (1974). Other important books are: *The Flea Circus* (1989), *City Beat* (1991), and *Senryu Magazine* (2001). *Baseball Poems,* a sequence of nine baseball haiku and senryu, came out as a folded broadside in 1988.

In 1964, Alan helped restart the St. Lucy C.Y.O. baseball team in Newark, for which his Uncle Rocco Pizzarelli had played first base in 1948. Alan's team won its league championship and he received the Sportsmanship Award. He played centerfield, his favorite position, but also pitched and played first. Alan throws lefty and is a switch-hitter.

at the produce stand
a kid with a baseball
plays catch with the awning

leaning for the sign
the pitcher rotates the ball
behind his back

struck out —
    back in the dugout
        he kicks the water cooler

at shortstop
between innings
sparrows dust-bathing

game over
all the empty seats
turn blue

the score keeper
peeks out of the scoreboard
spring rain

leaving the game
the click of his cleats
fade into the clubhouse

bases loaded —
at the crack of the bat
the crowd pops up

7th inning stretch
the facade's shadow reaches
the pitcher's mound

saturday afternoon
as the ballgame ends
geese return to the outfield

october rain
the tarpaulin ripples
across the infield

Brenda Gannam 1950

Brenda Gannam writes: "An early interest in baseball began in high school when I attended local team (Class A) games with my friends. Later, during my marriage to a Brooklyn artist and poet who was a great fan of the Dodgers and who grew up next door to Ebbets Field, I learned some of the finer points of the game—and was attracted to its Zen-like qualities. I'm a fan of the Atlanta Braves (being from Georgia) and the New York Yankees (having lived in New York for the past twenty-five years)."

Gannam was born April 19, 1950, in Savannah and lived there until the age of eighteen. She went to the University of Georgia; the Université de Dijon in France, The Johns Hopkins School of Advanced International Studies in Washington, and the American University in Cairo, Egypt, acquiring along the way a BA in French Language and Literature and an MA in International Affairs/Middle East.

She first learned about haiku ("you know, 5-7-5") in a high-school English class. She never thought about trying to write them until the early '90s when a friend active in New York poetry circles said her poetry had a haiku-like quality. In 1996 Gannam joined The Haiku Society of America. She has served as Regional Coordinator for HSA, was on the planning committee for the 2003 Haiku North America conference in New York, and for the past several years has been the coordinator of The Spring Street Haiku Group. Though she writes haiku and senryu on a variety of subjects, those about dating, romance, and sex are among her most popular. She even finds them at the ballpark.

having an affair
with his buddy's wife
the DH

new girlfriend
safe
at first

handsome pitcher
my eyes drift down
to the mound

home team rally
outside the stadium
the roar of Harley engines

slow, high fly
somewhere down the line
the whistle of a train

end of the inning
the umpire counting something
on his fingers

in the stands
his arm around his wife
he winks at me

stealing third
over the loudspeaker
the security firm's ad

fastball
the pitcher slyly adjusts
his equipment

Mike Dillon 1950

Born on May 29, 1950, in Seattle, Washington, Mike Dillon grew up on Bainbridge Island, eight miles west across the water from Seattle. "By the time I reached the University of Washington in 1969," Dillon writes, "my formal athletic career was over. I pitched a no-hitter in my first little league game, a moment of bliss I experienced again thirty-seven years later when Edgar Martinez doubled Ken Griffey Jr. home from first base to win the fifth and final game of the 1995 playoff series between the Seattle Mariners and New York Yankees.

"As a little leaguer and for a few years beyond, I pitched and played first base. I throw left and bat right. I also write haiku and 'regular' poetry. I like the Pacific Northwest rain and sunshine when it happens. I live in a small town on Puget Sound, Indianola, and commute to Seattle where I publish a half-dozen community newspapers. I was first exposed to haiku in 1960 when my third-grade teacher put some haiku by Dag Hammarskjöld up on the blackboard. In the mid-1980s the work of Sam Hamill led me to Asian poetry and eventually haiku. It felt like a kind of homecoming.

"My first haiku was published in *Modern Haiku* in February 1988 and I have been a regular contributer to *Modern Haiku* and other haiku magazines ever since. I have one book of haiku in print, *The Road Behind*, from Red Moon Press."

> cold motel window:
> faraway in the dusk
> a softball game

the last kid picked
running his fastest
to right field

Tom Painting 1951

Tom Painting was born on April 1, 1951, in Rochester, New York, where he lives and works as a middle and high school English and creative writing teacher. The oldest of six children, he was taught to play and love baseball at an early age by a father who, until he got married, had played semipro baseball. "Some of my fondest memories as a kid," the poet writes, "are of the choose-up sandlot games my friends and I would arrange after school and on weekends. We'd play for endless hours, without adult intervention, amending the rules, settling our own disputes, and creating high drama. I played the outfield, threw and batted left-handed, and often led off in the batting lineup. I followed the exploits of the '60s Yankees: Maris, Mantle, Berra, Richardson, etc. I was a Yankee fan to the core and am to this day." A gifted runner, Painting concentrated on track events while in high school and college, so wasn't involved with organized ball until his twenties when he began playing for an amateur softball team. He loves the outdoors and is an avid bird-watcher who has identified 594 North American species.

About haiku, Painting writes, "I first came to haiku about twelve years ago, when a friend of mine gave me as a birthday gift, a subscription to the [haiku] journal *Brussels Sprout*. I was intrigued. I wrote one haiku, which was accepted and published. Easy I thought. It was at least a year before I wrote another 'keeper,' and by then I had come to realize the meaning of beginner's luck. Haiku takes practice and discipline, just like baseball."

all day rain
on the playing field
a stray dog

bases loaded
a full moon clears
the right field fence

the foul ball lands
in an empty seat
summer's end

Tom Clausen 1951

A lifelong resident of Ithaca, New York, Tom Clausen was born there on August 1, 1951, and graduated in 1973 from Cornell University. He presently works in the university library and plays outfield for the library's ball club, called the Stacks Rats, in a recreational softball league. He throws and bats right-handed. Clausen is a fan of the St. Louis Cardinals. He picked them as *his* team almost randomly at the start of the 1967 season. His choice was based, he says, "on the team's name, and on its location." Being between the North and South and between East and West and right on the "Big Muddy," it seemed a perfect location for a team that would represent for him America's pastime: "The Cardinals won the World Series that year and I became a lifelong fan. My favorite players at the time were Lou Brock and Bob Gibson."

He first learned of haiku in the early 1980s when a friend gave him one of the four volumes of R. H. Blyth's *Haiku*. He didn't seriously take it up though until 1988 after he read an article in an Ithaca newspaper about Ruth Yarrow, a haiku poet then living in the area. His first haiku was "published in *Modern Haiku* in 1988 or 1989 and was written in Ithaca after viewing ducks on a winter day on Cayuga Lake."

He is part of a small haiku group, which also includes John Stevenson, called the Route 9 Haiku Group. It meets several times a year in a Chinese restaurant in Halfmoon, New York, and publishes an annual chapbook of haiku titled *Upstate Dim Sum*. His latest book, *being there,* was recently published by Swamp Press.

in the shoe box
attic light from one window
and the creased Willie Mays

from the train window
fans outside the ballpark
before the game

back to back walks . . .
the catcher takes the pitcher
to the top of the mound

bottom of the 8th
eight determined drunks
get the wave going . . .

full moon just rising
we recount the best plays
on the drive home

Jim Kacian 1953

Jim Kacian, besides being an accomplished haiku poet is one of the most important editors and publishers of the genre in English. From 1997 through 2004, he was editor of *Frogpond,* the journal of the Haiku Society of America, and his Red Moon Press is one of the most innovative and productive haiku presses in the world. His own books have been published in the United States and abroad: *Out of the Stones: Selected Haiku of Jim Kacian,* was brought out in 2001 by a publisher in Slovenia. A force in international haiku, he has toured the world on its behalf.

Kacian was born on July 26, 1953, in Worcester, Massachusetts, and raised in nearby Gardner. He remembers writing his first poem in 1968. His experience with baseball began much earlier. "I have played baseball for as long as I can remember," he writes. "It was my first sport, first organized activity outside the house, first passion. I had a glove from the time I was six years old, and listened on the radio to the games of my favorite team, the Boston Red Sox. The baseball diamond at Jackson Playground was a hundred yards from my house, and I grew up there."

Kacian played in park leagues from seven into his teens, playing all positions. At fourteen he was invited by the Red Sox to participate in an Instructional League Camp. Before he was to go, an accident during practice resulted in a misunderstanding with a park league instructor that caused Kacian to drop out of league play, turn down the Red Sox offer, and to take up the game of tennis. He became a skilled tennis player and had a brief career on the professional circuit in the 1970s.

calm evening
the ballgame play-by-play
across the water

called third strike —
the slow roll of the ball
back to the mound

seventh-inning stretch —
dust from dragging the bases
hangs in the air

October revival
all hands lift
to the foul ball

gathering the balls
with the last light
season's end

Ed Markowski 1954

Ed Markowski, the son of a steel-worker father and a kindergarten-teaching Italian mother, was born April 14, 1954, in a hospital in Detroit about a mile from Tiger Stadium. He first learned about haiku in 1967 when his older sister brought a book home called *The Four Seasons* (1958). Published by The Peter Pauper Press, it was a small book of Japanese haiku in seventeen-syllable English translations by Peter Beilenson. Markowski, impressed by haiku's "eloquent simplicity," treasured the book. He still has it.

He didn't try writing haiku until 1989, when he wrote fifty-five of them "still under the illusion of the seventeen-syllable rule." After discovering William J. Higginson's *The Haiku Handbook* (1985) a short time later, he began to write with a freer and more knowledgeable hand. His first published haiku appeared in *bottle rockets* in 2001. His first chapbook, *Pop-Up*, came out in 2004 in vince tripi's Pinchbook series.

Markowski's other interests include family (he and his wife, Laurice, have a daughter and grandson), cooking, film, music, basketball, politics, psychology, Buddhism, cats, and especially baseball. He pitched for the St. Sylvester Darts in 1967 and 1968: "In '68, I went 13 & 2. From 1985 to '87 I played right field for, and managed, a slow-pitch team of drunks and misfits called The Cuban Heels. I throw right, and switch hit."

His all-time favorite team is the '76 Tigers of Mark Fidrych and Ron Leflore. The "most memorable game" he ever attended: Denny McLain's thirtieth win of the 1968 season. His favorite player ever: Luis Tiant.

winter reverie
the faint scent of bubblegum
on an old baseball card

spring snow . . .
in the empty garage
a boy works on his swing

sides chosen
the boy not chosen
lends me his glove

afternoon heat . . .
the lazy dip
of a palm ball

summer loneliness
dropping the pop-up
i toss to myself

distant thunder
the home run hitter
drops a bunt

rainy night
a hole in the radio
where a ballgame should be

73 dingers?
everytime i see his smile
on the Wheaties box

box scores
the taste
of a breakfast sausage

summer haze
i pick off
the invisible man on first

signs of autumn
his bunt dies
at the five yard line

another cold front . . .
i oil
my glove

hot stove league . . .
did ryan's fastball
cast a shadow?

spring training . . .
flamingoes graze
on the mansion lawn

bases loaded
the rookie pitcher
blows a bubble

chattanooga . . .
the left fielder drifts
in the shadow of a mountain

Fourth of July . . .
the glow
of stadium lights

rising into thunderclouds
the umpire's
right arm

late innings
the shortstop backpedals
into fireflies

night game in durango
all the stars
above the diamond

late september . . .
dry leaves rattle
on the chain-link backstop

Randy Brooks 1954

Randy Brooks is Chair of the English Department at Millikin University in Decatur, Illinois, where he also oversees what is undoubtedly the best English-language haiku program of any school in the country. He and his wife, Shirley Brooks, have been the owners and editors of the influential haiku press Brooks Books (originally called High/Coo Press) since 1976. They also publish *Mayfly* magazine. Among Brooks's own books are *School's Out: Selected Haiku of Randy Brooks* (Press Here, 1999) and *The Homestead Cedars* (Saki Press, 1999).

The poet was born on June 18, 1954, in Hutchinson, Kansas, and grew up in western Kansas. As a boy, he played little league: "with shortstop as my favorite position, although I also played outfield because I could throw it in. I throw right and bat right." When his sons were young he coached little league for a couple of years. His daughter plays softball now and he tries "to remain calm from the stands."

Here is Brooks on how he first learned about haiku: "My senior year at Ball State University I won the literary award for poetry and bought several poetry books with my prize money including *The Haiku Anthology*. My senior thesis had been a history of Greek lyric poetry and its influence on short English poetry, so I had already seen connections to haiku while working on that. Then at Purdue University [tanka poet] Sandy Goldstein was one of my poetry mentors, teaching me about tanka and reluctantly helping me with my haiku. I also started corresponding with Ray Roseliep at that time, so he became my haiku mentor."

carrying his glove
the boy's dog follows him
to the baseball field

opening day . . .
green of the field
through the ticket gates

baseball
rolls into the mud —
painted lady flutters up

last day of school . . .
the crack of a baseball bat
through an open window

thunder . . .
little leaguers chatter
silenced

Michael Ketchek 1954

Michael Ketchek was born on July 9, 1954, in Detroit, Michigan, a first generation American of a German mother and Armenian father. He has lived since 1955 in Rochester, New York, except for brief periods in Missouri and Portland, Maine, after college. He received a BA in political science from SUNY at Purchase, New York, in 1977. He and his wife of sixteen years have a twelve-year-old son.

He writes: "I am a daycare teacher, prefer dark beer, go for lots of walks in the woods, and politically am a radical and pacifist. I learned about haiku in the third grade from my teacher in Rochester Public School #46. About the same time, I became a baseball and Yankee fan when I saw Mickey Mantle on TV hit a home run off Barney Schultz in the 1964 World Series. I'm still a Yankee fan though I also root for the Tigers since I was born in Detroit. As a kid we played a lot of softball, often with only three or four on a team. I throw and bat right-handed. We also played hotbox on our dead-end street and in the fall lots of touch football.

"My brother and I would play catch—with grounders and fly balls—and Wiffle Ball in the driveway. We also liked a card and dice game called Strat-O-Matic baseball. My brother and I still get together once a week to play it. (Last week the 1927 Yankees split a pair of games with the '36 Yanks. Waite Hoyt got a shutout in the first game.) My son and I have gone to see major league games in Detroit, Philadelphia, Cleveland, Baltimore, Chicago, and Toronto. My wife, son, and I also frequently see the local Rochester Red Wings play."

forsythia
the sound of a ball
striking a bat

summer night radio
thru the dark static
a Pedro fastball

Wiffle Ball —
a windblown home run
over the neighbor's Rambler

dog days of summer
twenty-three games
out of first

struck out
the long walk home
in the dusk

Bruce Kennedy 1957

Bruce Kennedy was born December 29, 1957, in Toledo, Ohio, raised in the suburbs of northern New Jersey, and now lives in Brooklyn. Besides baseball and haiku, his interests include backpacking, photography, and zen. He is a practicing Buddhist.

He writes: "The first haiku I came upon were quoted in Alan Watts' book *The Way of Zen,* which I read as a sophomore in high school. My high school and town libraries were pretty good and I was able to read R. H. Blyth's books, Harold G. Henderson, and a translation of Bashō's *Monkey's Raincoat.* My English teacher even did a class on haiku. I wrote my first haiku as a junior in high school about an inchworm in my backyard. Midway through college I began to write and publish haiku in earnest, and was briefly editor of the Haiku Society of America's magazine *Frogpond* my senior year.

"As for baseball, I played right field in little league. I threw and batted right-handed and was not very good. I'm not sure I even finished the season. This is ironic because my grandfather's life was baseball. He ran an American Legion team in Western Pennsylvania for twenty-six years, leading his team to the state playoffs thirteen times and winning seven. He helped several miners' children get baseball scholarships to college, and was a scout with the Detroit Tigers. He was so beloved that in 2003 over one hundred of his former players held a banquet in his honor and rededicated a local ballpark in his name. I've been a Mets fan since I moved to Brooklyn. This haiku was written at the KeySpan stadium in Coney Island, home of the Mets' triple-A team, The Cyclones."

blue sky
I buy a ticket
to a minor league game

Michael Dylan Welch 1962

Michael Dylan Welch was born on May 20, 1962, in Watford, England, where cricket, rather than baseball, is the pastime. As a child in England, he played "rounders," a sport vaguely like baseball. It wasn't until he was a teenager, living in Canada, that he began to play baseball. Around the same time he learned about haiku in English class. He writes that he never excelled at any particular position in baseball, but does remember once being knocked out by a girl who hit a ball straight between his eyes when he was pitching in a pick-up game.

In addition to writing and publishing haiku and other literary works, Welch has been an officer of the Haiku Society of America, founded the Tanka Society of America (and served as its president for five years), cofounded the American Haiku Archives at the California State Library in Sacramento, and cofounded the Haiku North America conferences, which began in 1991 and continue to take place every other year. He currently works as an editor for the Microsoft Web site. He also edits and publishes *Tundra: The Journal of the Short Poem* and heads Press Here, a publisher of haiku and tanka books. After sixteen years in California, he moved in 2003 to Sammamish, Washington, near Seattle, where he enjoys watching Seattle Mariners baseball games. He and his wife, Hiromi, have a son, Thomas Taiyo Welch, born in October 2003.

> base hit —
> the outfielder's
> four shadows

first drops of rain —
    puffs of dust
rise from the infield

Dan McCullough 1966

Growing up in Maine, Dan McCullough became a Red Sox fan early in life: "Baseball and by extension, Wiffle Ball, were large parts of my childhood, but what really took hold were the 1975 Boston Red Sox. I wanted to be #19, Fred Lynn, playing center and making diving catches. I begged my parents to let me stay up to watch Game 6 of the Series that year. What I felt after the game was pure joy. Less than twenty-four hours later I was heartbroken. This was a recurring theme up until 2004." McCullough played third base for his junior high team after three years in little league. "Since then," he writes, "the pull baseball has over me hasn't lessened—whether its the sight of the local ballfield covered in snow, or the memory of my blue mitt." He "still tries to play a few innings of Wiffle Ball" when he can.

The poet was born on January 6, 1966, in Old Orchard Beach, Maine, a coastal town with a large amusement area, including a roller-coaster and a long pier crowded with games of chance, food stalls, and souvenir stands. Lively in summer, it is quiet in the winter. He graduated from the University of Maine in 1989 and now lives in Massachusetts, where he works as a naturalist for the Audubon Society. McCullough began writing haiku in 2000 after being inspired by the work of the Japanese haiku poet Chiyo-ni. Though most of his early writing focused on subjects from his hometown, such as bumper cars and seagulls, his first haiku was on baseball: "Spring shares its welcome / with an AM radio — / Opening Day." His haiku were featured in Red Moon Press's *A New Resonance 3* (2001).

entering
the batter's box
afternoon shadows

during
the pitching change
cicadas

darkening clouds
the umpire's voice
quickens

first lightning
the shortstop
flashes leather

staring in
the closer shakes off
the rain

rain delay
puddles on the infield tarp
widening

shooting star . . .
promptly picked off
second base

during
the pop-up
full moon

above
the bartender's head
Game 7

Mathew V. Spano 1967

Born on November 22, 1967, in Summit, New Jersey, Mathew V. Spano grew up in Hillsborough, NJ. He was introduced to baseball by his father who "played semi-pro for the New York Giants, hit against Satchel Paige, and shook Babe Ruth's hand." Mathew played little league, but says he "mostly grew up playing Wiffle Ball with my brothers in our suburban backyard. We played fast pitch, used a baseball bat instead of a plastic one, and for a backstop we stood an old wheelbarrow on end with the handles facing skyward. I remember the 'CLANG!' that accompanied each strike. We also played softball in the street with the neighborhood kids, and unintention-ally broke our neighbors' windows, dented their garbage cans, and fractured the tail lights on their cars. We had very compassionate neighbors. Recently, I started a soft-ball team at the college where I work. I play center field and hit third in the lineup." As a kid he liked the New York Yankees: "We didn't go to many games, but we watched them on TV and listened to Phil Rizzuto and Bill White. My favorite players were Ron Guidry and, later, Don Mattingly."

Spano learned about haiku in grammar school and again in graduate school. His first published haiku appeared in 1996 in *The Piedmont Literary Review*, his first baseball haiku in 2005 in *Modern Haiku*. He received a PhD in comparative literature from Rutgers University and now teaches at Middlesex County College in Edison, NJ. He and his wife have two chil-dren and besides playing ball and writing haiku, he likes hiking, fly-fishing, and playing the piano.

alone
in the autumn night
the home run ball

late afternoon
the pitcher's curveball drops
into the shadows

radio static
somewhere in the muggy night
a ballgame

the dark stadium
moths and fans disperse
into the night

a chill wind
whistles through the bleachers
the locked equipment box

Chad Lee Robinson 1980

Chad Lee Robinson was born on July 8, 1980, in Pierre, South Dakota, and grew up there on the banks of the Missouri River. As a kid he played along with his older brother and some cousins in little league. He usually played right field, but he says "I always preferred a game of catch." He throws and bats right-handed.

He first learned about haiku in a creative writing class while at South Dakota State University, from which he graduated in 2003 with a BA in English. The class was taught by South Dakota State Poet Laureate, David Allan Evans. "I've been captivated by haiku/senryu ever since," writes Robinson. "I read everything I could find, which wasn't much, mainly *The Haiku Anthology* and *Haiku Moment*. I found some good info online that led me to the Haiku Society of America and the magazines *Frogpond, Modern Haiku,* and *The Heron's Nest,* and I went on from there. My first published haiku was in *Mayfly* 36, Winter 2003." He is one of the poets featured in Red Moon Press's *A New Resonance: Emerging Voices in English Language Haiku 4* (2005) and is a member of the Haiku Society of America and the Skipping Stones Haiku Group.

He still lives in Pierre.

> long summer day —
> spoke by spoke the baseball card
> loses its rattle

dusk —
a ball field's lights
shining through the trees

JAPANESE

BASEBALL HAIKU

Masaoka Shiki (正岡 子規) 1867–1902

The last of the four great pillars of Japanese haiku and the first modern haiku poet, Masaoka Shiki revived the genre of haiku from its stagnant state near the end of the nineteenth century and gave it a new and vibrant life. Influenced by recent Western literature and art, he used common language and new subject matter to move haiku away from the classical vocabulary and conventional themes that had been stifling innovation. He wrote about glass doors, railroad trains, and even a new game—baseball. In 1890 he created the world's first baseball haiku. He had discovered baseball while going to a preparatory school in Tokyo where he played for the school team. In 1889 he brought a ball and bat back to his hometown of Matsuyama and taught the sport to his friends, introducing baseball to that area of Japan for the first time. For this, and for his haiku, tanka, and other writings on baseball, Shiki was elected to the Japanese Baseball Hall of Fame in 2002. When he played for his school team, his favorite position was that of catcher—even though he was left-handed.

spring breeze
this grassy field makes me
want to play catch

春風やまりを投げたき草の原

haru kaze ya   mari wo nagetaki   kusa no hara

the young grass
kids get together
to hit a ball

若草や子供集まりて毬を打つ

wakakusa ya   kodomo atsumarite   mari wo utsu

the trick
to ball catching
the willow in a breeze

球うける極秘は風の柳かな

tama ukeru   gokuhi wa kaze no   yanagi kana

like young cats
still ignorant of love
we play with a ball

恋知らぬ猫のふり也球あそび

koi shiranu   neko no furi nari   tama asobi

long grass
the baseball paths
are white

草茂みベースボールの道白し

kusa shigemi   bēsubōru no   michi shiroshi

summer grass
baseball players far off
in the distance

夏草やベースボールの人遠し

natsukusa ya   bēsubōru no   hito tōshi

dandelions
the baseball rolled
through them

蒲公英ヤボールコロゲテ通リケリ
tanpopo ya bōru korogete tōri keri

beyond the hedge
they are playing ball
in a withered field

生垣の外は枯野や球遊び

ikegaki no   soto wa kareno ya   tama-asobi

I'd like to play catch
in this public plaza
spring grass

まり投げて見たき広場や春の草

mari nagete mitaki hiroba ya haru no kusa

Kawahigashi Hekigotō (河東 碧梧桐) 1873–1937

Hekigotō was one of Shiki's most important disciples. After the master's death, he continued to support Shiki's emphasis on objectivity and went even further in the pursuit of innovation. He wrote many haiku without following the seventeen-syllable rule, writing some in twenty or more syllables. He promoted haiku "without a center of interest" and his haiku often have a bland, descriptive quality. His importance lies in the effect he had on the direction others were to take. He started the New Trend Haiku Movement, attracting such radical poets as Ogiwara Seisensui (1884–1976), who helped argue for the viability of dropping the traditional form. Seisensui wanted other changes and broke with Hekigotō. Rejecting the season-word requirement and advocating a move to more subjectivity in haiku, he attracted such modern free-verse haiku individualists as Hōsai and Santōka.

Born in Matsuyama, Hekigotō was friends with both Shiki and Takahama Kyoshi from the time they were still young. He had many other interests aside from his work as a haiku poet and critic. He was active as a calligrapher, mountain climber, classical scholar, and noh dancer, while still finding time to travel to, and to write travel essays about, North America, Europe, and China. Masaoka Shiki, besides being his haiku master, also taught him how to play baseball. In 1889, after he had discovered baseball at a school in Tokyo, Shiki brought a bat and ball back to Matsuyama for Hekigotō and taught him the game. Hekigotō apparently published only one baseball haiku, written in 1924.

while playing ball
it becomes time to go home
for supper

球遊んで居て夕飯に帰る頃

tama asonde   ite yūhan ni   kaeru koro

Mizuhara Shūōshi (水原　秋桜子) 1892–1981

Mizuhara Shūōshi was the eldest son of a doctor who ran a clinic in Tokyo. After getting his own medical degree in 1926, he began teaching at Showa Medical College and practicing in his father's clinic. In 1932 he became medical adviser to the Imperial Household, retiring from medicine twenty years later. He liked to visit Buddhist temples and to attend baseball games.

Shūōshi started writing poetry as a student, beginning with tanka and moving on to haiku. He became a follower of Kyoshi and the conservative branch of haiku. He continued to use the traditional form and seasonal reference after breaking with Kyoshi to form his own group, but leaned toward the lyrical and romantic. He believed one should use the imagination in haiku, and not just record objective observations of nature. He criticized Shiki's idea of word-sketching from nature, by ridiculing the image of a poet, notebook in hand, following after a cloud's shadow. His style involves being open to a wide range of subject matter and using theatrical or dramatic effects. His best haiku have a cinematic quality: "the huge dog / rises to greet the guest / May darkness." His baseball haiku also reflect this concern with action and mood to create drama.

> night game
> our team's good luck heralded
> by the lightning

ナイターやツキのはじめのはた〻神
naitā ya   tsuki no hajime no   hatatagami

a night game's
bright lights across
the great river

ナイターの光芒大河へだてけり

naitā no   kōbō   taiga   hedate keri

神宮球場風景

[Five] Scenes at Jingu Baseball Stadium

the siren starts the game
autumn sunlight breaks
through the clouds

サイレンの鳴るとき秋日雲を破る

sairen no   naru toki akihi   kumo wo yaburu

[In Japan a siren signals the start of a baseball game]

cheering fans
fly kites from the stadium
over the autumn garden

応援の凧こそあがれ苑の秋

ōen no   tako koso agare   en no aki

[Jingu Stadium is next to the Meiji Shrine and garden]

154

the player takes
his position in the outfield
a cricket's cry

外野手の守りに鳴ける虫あはれ

gaiyashu no   mamori ni nakeru   mushi aware

the grass so green
music booms across it from
the loudspeakers

青芝や楽を奏づる拡声器

aoshiba ya   gaku wo kanazuru   kakuseiki

evening glow
everyone looks up at
the winning team's waving flag

夕焼けし勝利の旗を皆仰ぐ

yūyakeshi   shōri no hata wo   mina aogu

Yamaguchi Seishi (山口 誓子) 1901–1994

Yamaguchi Seishi was born November 3, 1901, in Kyoto. He began writing haiku as a boy. In 1926 he graduated from Tokyo University with a law degree and began working for a commercial company in Osaka. He was sickly and had to take off from work quite often, sometimes for long periods. In the 1940s, in order to safeguard his health, he began to lead a retiring life, living in small towns on Honshu's Pacific coast.

With his first book, *Tōkō* (*Frozen Harbor*), published in 1932, and in the following years, Seishi led the avantgarde by using modern urban images and foreign words (in katakana) in his haiku. He broke with the traditionalist Kyoshi and joined Shūōshi's splinter group. He broke with them to form the Tenrō (Sirius) group, with Saitō Sanki (a progressively minded poet interested in baseball) as the editor of its magazine (1948). In Seishi's haiku, we find guns, trains, skyscrapers, and other elements of contemporary life. A well-known example is "in the summer grass / the wheels of a locomotive / come to a stop." Seishi also caught the resonance that can be found in the juxtaposition of simple things: "summer river / the end of a red iron chain / soaks in the water." He wrote haiku about many sports, including rugby, swimming, golf, and skating. Seishi saw his first night game in 1960 and wrote "watching the night game." His fascination with the magical world of night games mirrors his interest in modernity, particularly one of its most striking manifestations: bright lights.

the night game
at the bottom of the stadium
the brightest spot on earth

ナイターの底下界にて最も明

naitā no   soko gekai nite   mottomo mei

the season's first night game
but you will not
be there

ナイターの始まる日にて君在らず

naitā no   hajimaru hi ni te   kimi arazu

[Written in 1962 in memory of Saitō Sanki]

watching a night game
the ordinary ground of night turns
into enchanted ground

ナイターに見る夜の土不思議な土

naitā ni   miru yoruno tsuchi   fushigina tsuchi

the same night's
two night games
separate worlds

同じ夜の両つナイター関らず

onajiyo no   futatsu naitā   kakawarazu

a black ballplayer
the night game only just
lights him up

黒人の選手ナイターただ明るし

kokujin no   senshu naitā   tada akarushi

Akimoto Fujio (秋元 不死男) 1901–1977

Akimoto Fujio was born in Yokohama, Kanagawa Prefecture, on November 3, 1901, the same day Yamaguchi Seishi was born in Kyoto. After graduating from Higher Elementary School, he was employed by an insurance company in Yokohama, where he worked until 1940 as a clerk. He enrolled in night school in 1919 and began reading widely and writing novels and poems. He soon became committed to Marxism.

In 1934 he became friends with Saitō Sanki (1900–1962), a haiku poet and baseball fan. (A Sanki postwar haiku that mentions baseball: "after eating whalemeat / the orphans and the doctor / play baseball.") Fujio became more involved with haiku activities and wrote about Seishi's work in a 1939 review called "The Start of Modern Haiku: An Analysis of Seishi's Haiku." In 1940 he published his first book of haiku: *Machi* (*City*).

Fujio then began a new movement called "Emerging Haiku." His Marxist ideals seemed to the authorities to be reflected in his work and to be at odds with the war effort, so they put him in jail in 1941 for two years. In 1947, he helped establish the Gendai Haiku Kyōkai (The Modern Haiku Association) and the next year became a member of Seishi's haiku group Tenrō (Sirius). He became head of his own group Hyōkai (Frozen Sea) in 1949 and five years later published an important article entitled "Haiku Mono Setsu" ("Haiku is Realistic"). He became Director General of the Haijin Kyōkai (The Haiku Poets Asssociation) in 1972.

This haiku contrasts the ballgame with the stillness of a pond where a turtle's shell reflects the distant light.

in the far sky
the lights of a night game
a turtle drying off

遠空にナイター明り亀乾く

tōzora ni   naitā akari   kame kawaku

Taki Shun'ichi (瀧 春一) 1902–1996

Taki Kumataro (he would later take the literary name Shun'ichi) was born on October 15, 1902, in Yokohama. In 1926 he became a member of Mizuhara Shūōshi's haiku group. Shūōshi originally came from the conservative Kyoshi's group, but he had broken with it to start his own group Ashibi (Japanese Andromeda). Calling for more imagination in haiku, he still supported the traditional form and the season-word requirement. Shun'ichi did well under Shūōshi and in 1933 became a *dojin,* a rank close to the leader. He then became a selector for *Hishi no Hana* (*Water Chestnut Blossoms*), a magazine for an associate group.

In 1940 this group changed its name to Danryu (Warm Current) and Shun'ichi became its president. He had become more liberal and began to advocate muki haiku, or haiku without a season word. This led to a break with Shūōshi in 1947. However, in 1966 he returned to Ashibi and a less radical position.

Shun'ichi's first *kushū* (haiku collection), *Kaya* (*Miscanthus Grass*), was published in 1935. In 1982 he was given the 16th Dakotsu Shō, a major haiku award named for haiku poet Iida Dakotsu.

> watching the night game
> someday, I too, may suffer
> a losing streak

ナイター観る吾が身もいつか負けがこむ
naitā miru   wagami mo itsuka   make ga komu

my office briefcase
I hold it tightly in my arms
as I watch the night game

勤の鞄しかと抱へてナイター観る
tsutome no kaban   shikato kakaete   naitā miru

Ozawa Seiyūshi (小沢 青柚子) 1912–1945

Ozawa Seiyūshi was born Ozawa Hideo on May 30, 1912, in Tokyo. He later took the pen name Seiyūshi, which means "Green Chinese Lemon." After graduating from Waseda University's Teachers College, he became a teacher at a girls' high school in Tokyo's Adachi Ward. In haiku circles, he was at an early stage of his career a dojin in the Ku to Hyōron (Haiku and Review) haiku group, but in 1937 left them to form his own group Kaze (Wind). Only a year later he returned to a reorganized Ku to Hyōron, bringing with him the major members of Kaze. The new combined group was called the Hiroba (Agora, or Public Plaza) Group.

Seiyūshi's "home run ball" haiku appeared in the *Modern Haiku Anthology* in 1941. His haiku have been described favorably by critics as "poetic." Here is an example: "a town in May / I hide out inside / my eye patch" (*machi gogatsu gantai no uchini waga kakure*). He may have been wearing an eye patch due to an injury and felt somehow he was seeing his inner self with the eye hidden by the patch. Another haiku by this poet: "the autumn wind / it is instantly a bare tree / high and sharp" (*akikaze wa tatoeba takaku toki raboku*).

He went to China during the war in 1941 and died there on December 11, 1945. Not much else seems to be known about him. Like his home run ball, he appeared and then was gone.

the autumn sky
appearing and falling away
a home run ball

秋天に見えて落ち行く本塁打

shū-ten ni   miete ochi-yuku   honruida

Kadokawa Genyoshi (角川　源義) 1917–1975

Kadokawa Genyoshi was born October 9, 1917, in Toyama Prefecture. When he was in the second year of junior high school, he became interested in writing haiku and in 1932 started submitting them to a haiku group. He entered Kokugakuin University in 1937 and majored in Japanese literature and folklore. In 1945, he established Kadokawa Shoten, a publishing company. (His son Kadakawa Haruki, also a haiku poet and a famous producer of films, took over the company at his father's death and built it into a multimedia giant.)

In 1952, Genyoshi founded *Haiku* magazine and began to preside over the haiku group Kawa (River). He stressed the importance of lyricism in haiku, feeling that it had been slighted after World War II. He received a PhD in Japanese literature in 1961. About the same time he was instrumental in arranging for the foundation of Haijin Kyōkai (the Haiku Poets Association) and later on helped start the Museum of Haiku Literature in Tokyo.

He established the Kadokawa Haiku/Tanka Award around 1960 and created the Dakotsu Award in 1962. He especially admired the haiku poets Iida Dakotsu (1885–1962) and Ishida Hakyō (1913–1969). Genyoshi died on October 27, 1975.

His haiku collection *Saigyō no Hi* (*Saigyō's Day*), published in 1975, was awarded the Yomiuri Bungaku Shō (the Yomiuri Literary Prize). Other books of haiku by this author are *Rodan no Kubi* (*Rodin's Head*) 1956, *Kamigami no Utage* (*Feast of the Gods*) 1969, and *Fuyu no Niji* (*Winter Rainbow*) 1972.

lights-out siren
the night game continues
by moonlight

消燈サイレン月のナイターなほつづく
shōtō sairen   tsuki no naitā   nao tsuzuku

Suzuki Murio (鈴木 六林男) 1919–2004

Suzuki Murio is one of the most famous gendai (modern) haiku poets. He sometimes wrote muki haiku (haiku without a season word). Born in Osaka in 1919, he became a professor and taught at Osaka University of Arts in the Literary Arts Department. He studied haiku with Saitō Sanki (who also wrote a haiku about orphans playing baseball). Murio became the leader of the Kayō (Bright Blossoms) haiku group in 1971. He received a number of gendai haiku awards, but also was given a Dakotsu Award for his haiku.

Here is one of his modern-style haiku: *ihin ari iwanami-bunko "Abe ichizoku."* In translation it is: "Left by the deceased — / only a paperback copy of / *The Family Abe*." (*The Family Abe* is a famous novel by Ogai Mori.)

Murio wrote the "orphans playing baseball" haiku when he was around the age of thirty, so the orphans in the poem probably lost their parents during World War II. It is from his volume *Tanima no Hata* (*A Flag in the Valley*), published in 1955. The "outfielder" haiku originally appeared in his *Akuryō* (*Apollyon,* or *Angel of Hell*), which came out in 1985.

Murio passed away in December 2004.

> My legs are chilly
> I stand watching the orphans
> play baseball

脚冷えて立ちて見ていし孤児の野球
ashi hiete tachite miteishi koji no yakyu

Over
the outfielder's loneliness —
the summer moon

外野手の孤独にかかり夏の月

gaiyashu no   kodoku ni kakari   natsu no tsuki

Yamazaki Hisao (山崎 ひさを) 1927

Yamazaki Hisao was born on November 29, 1927, in Tokyo. He studied haiku under Kishi Fusanro, who had been a follower of Yamaguchi Seishi. Hisao was employed at NHK television and is now both vice president of the Haiku Poets Association (Haijin Kyōkai) and the executive director of the Haiku International Association (HIA). He also heads the haiku group *Seizan* (*Green Mountain*) and its magazine of the same name.

An example of Hisao's haiku on other subjects than baseball is the following favorite: "autumn wind — / wetting the gravestone / the name appears" (*akikaze ya nurashite haka no moji ukabu*). When paying one's respects at some gravesites, you can take water with a dipper from a rectangular stone basin (like a shelf with water in it) at the base of the gravestone and pour it on the stone to purify and clean it. The wind dries the face of the stone first and the still wet incisions of the carved letters are darker and stand out. In the poem, the name appears almost magically, summoned by the autumn wind.

Among Hisao's books are *Jinnan* (1984) and *Hayakunin Cho* (1991). The "scorecard" haiku is from his book *Seizansho* (*Green Mountain Notes*), published by Furansudo (Chōfu City) in 2004. It had originally appeared in *Shinkiyose* (*New Saijiki*), published by Kagyusha (Tokyo), in 1995.

spilled ice
has wet the edge
of the scorecard

かちわりやスコアブックの端濡らし

kachiwari ya   sukoabukku no   hashi nurashi

Arima Akito (有馬 朗人) 1930

A world-class nuclear physicist and major haiku poet, Dr. Arima Akito was born in Japan on September 13, 1930. He graduated from Tokyo University in 1953, got his PhD there in 1958, and from 1989 to 1993 served as the university's president. He was president of Japan's Institute of Physical and Chemical Research from 1993 to 1998 and was his country's Minister of Education, Science, Sports, and Culture from 1998 to 2000. He has been a member of the upper house of the Japanese Diet (equivalent to the U.S. Senate) since 1998.

Dr. Arima's haiku mentor was Yamaguchi Seison (1892–1988). He joined Seison's haiku group when he was twenty years old. Because of his scientific profession he has traveled widely and many of his haiku reflect his experiences from around the world. His haiku collection *Ten'i* (*Providence*) received the Haiku Poets Association Prize for 1987. He started his own haiku group Ten'i in 1990. In 1995, Dr. Arima played a role in arranging for a delegation of important Japanese haiku poets to go to Chicago to take part in the first joint conference of the Japan-based Haiku International Association and the Haiku Society of America. He is presently honorary president of the HIA, has chaired the Masaoka Shiki International Haiku Prize selection commitee, and in other ways has helped to encourage the reading and writing of haiku throughout the world.

The ballpark mentioned in the poem is Kōshien Stadium near Osaka where the Japan high school baseball finals are held each year. It is also the home of the Central League's Hanshin Tigers.

Kōshien Stadium:
at the same moment a swallow
and a cool breeze

甲子園一瞬燕と涼風と

kōshien   isshun tsubame to   ryōfū to

Takaha Shugyō (鷹羽 狩行) 1930

Born in Yamagata Prefecture on October 5, 1930, Takaha Shugyō grew up in Onomichi, Hiroshima Prefecture, and began writing haiku when he was fifteen years old. He graduated from Chūou University, concentrating on literature and the law. Takaha started studying with the haiku master Yamaguchi Seishi in 1948 and then with Akimoto Fujio beginning in 1954. He formed his own haiku group, Kari (Hunting), in 1978, and became president of the Association of Haiku Poets (Haijin Kyōkai) in 2002. He is an adviser to the Haiku International Association (Kokusai Haiku Kōryū Kyōkai) and a director of the Japan Writers' Association. He has published more than a dozen volumes of haiku in Japanese (two with English translations) and many anthologies and books of essays. Takaha's first book of haiku was *Tanjō* (*Birth*) published in 1965. For it, he was awarded the Haijin Kyōkai Sho (the Association of Haiku Poets Prize) and the Minister of Education's Young Poets Award. A professional poet, he makes his living by teaching, judging, and creating haiku. It has been estimated that as judge and editor, he reads on average about 30,000 haiku a month.

night game
the black pitcher's
invincible

ナイターの黒人投手打ち崩せず

naitā no   kokujin-tōshu   uchi-kuzusezu

night game
the grass so thick and smooth
I want to step on it

ナイターの芝の緻密を踏みたけれ

naitā no　shiba no chimitsu wo　fumi-takere

Hoshino Tsunehiko (星野 恒彦) 1935

Hoshino Tsunehiko was born in Tokyo on November 19, 1935. A professor emeritus of English literature and comparative literature at Waseda University, Hoshino leads the haiku group Ten (Marten). He serves as the executive director of the Association of Haiku Poets and works as the director of the International Division for the Museum of Haiku Literature in Tokyo. He is also vice president of the Haiku International Association. Partly because of these positions and his work in translating Japanese haiku into English, Hoshino is well known among haiku poets all around the world.

He has published three collections of haiku: *Rendako, Bakushu,* and *Kantan.* He has also produced two collections of essays: *Haiku to Haiku no Sekai (The World of Haiku and Non-Japanese Haiku)*, which received the Association of Haiku Poets Award for Criticism in 2002, and *Shiku no Mori o Yuku (Strolling in the Woods of Haiku and Poetry)*. He has also published numerous articles, haiku, and translations in magazines, newspapers, and on the Web.

His baseball haiku about his son is a celebration of life. The boy, nature, and the game of baseball are all "budding" with the spring day.

my son runs toward
the budding tree —
their first base

芽吹く樹が一塁ベース吾子走る

mebuku ki ga ichirui-bēsu ako hashiru

Imai Sei (今井 聖) 1950

Imai Sei was born on October 12, 1950, in Niigata Prefecture on the coast of the Japan Sea. He attended a high school in Tottori Prefecture. His school's baseball team went to the national finals at Kōshien Stadium near Osaka. He was not on the team but he has "a lot of memories" about high school baseball. He belonged to the school's kendo (Japanese fencing) club. When he went to college he took English literature courses and studied Ezra Pound and Imagism. He now lives in Yokohama where he teaches high school.

He joined the Kanrai (Winter Thunder) haiku group in 1971 and was awarded the group's haiku prize in 1981. Imai is also interested in the cinema and in 1995 wrote the script for the film *Asian Blue*. He is a haiku selector for the *Tokyo Shinbun* (*Tokyo Newspaper*), Kanagawa region, and is a member of the Association of Haiku Poets. Imai now has his own haiku group called Machi (City), where he stresses the importance of the *shasei* (sketching from nature) method of writing haiku, originally taught by Masaoka Shiki. The poet sketches in words what he observes in nature, then turns these notes into finished haiku.

Yokohama High School, where he teaches English, has also played in the finals at Kōshien and has produced many professional baseball players, a number of whom have made the majors. One of these, a pitcher named Matsuzaka, was called "Monster" for his power. He now plays in Seibu for a Pacific League team and is still quite popular. So one way Imai can feel close to the world of baseball is through his students.

from the classroom
one can see the baseball field
spring clouds

教室から見ゆる球場春の雲

kyōshitsu kara   miyuru kyūjō   haru no kumo

the baseball stadium's
ten-thousand empty seats
the first swallow

球場に万の空席初燕
kyūjō ni   man no kūseki   hatsu-tsubame

it's the time of year
for night games to begin
eggplants in flower

ナイターの始まる頃の茄子の花
naitā no   hajimaru koro no   nasu no hana

at the night game
seeing a former pupil
in the bleachers

教へ子に遭ふナイターの外野席
oshiego ni   au naitā no   gaiya-seki

after the error
the player still faces the outfield
towering clouds

エラーしてまだ後ろ向き雲の峰

erā shite   mada ushiro-muki   kumo no mine

the lizard disappears
while the little league catcher
keeps crying out loud

いつまでも捕手号泣す蜥蜴消え
itsumademo   hoshu gōkyūsu   tokage kie

walking home
with his glove on his head
shrieking cicadas

グロウブを頭に乗せて蟬時雨
guroubu wo   atama ni nosete   semi-shigure

a ground-rule double
any ball that's hit into
the green onion field

二塁打とせり葱畑に入りたるは
nirui-da to   seri negi-batake ni   iritaru wa

the baseball thrown
back into the game is wet
a mackerel sky

返球の濡れてゐたりし鰯雲

henkyū no   nurete itarashi   iwashigumo

Yotsuya Ryū (四ツ谷 龍) 1958

Born on June 13, 1958, in Hokkaido, Yotsuya Ryū is known as both a haiku poet and a haiku, art, and movie critic. He first encountered haiku at ten in his Japanese class in elementary school. He was soon reading haiku guides ("how to books") by Nakamura Kusatao and Kusumoto Kenkichi, and a saijiki (haiku almanac) edited by Mizuhara Shūōshi. In 1974 Yotsuya joined the haiku group Taka (Hawk), headed by Fujita Shōshi (b. 1926). Shōshi demonstrates in his haiku a sensitive approach to the momentary details of nature: "deep in the mountains / thin ice on spring puddles / fades like the blossoms." Ryū also admired the avant-garde work of Nakatsuka Ippekirō (1887–1946) and tried writing free-style haiku. His university graduation thesis was on the French poet Guillaume Apollinaire (1880–1918), who was a major influence on the surrealists, both poets and artists. Yotsuya published his first haiku collection *Jiai* (*Charity*) in 1987. He has written a series of articles about haiku for a French poetry magazine and in 2001 he gave presentations on the subject of "What kind of poem is haiku?" in Bulgaria and Hungary. A revised second edition of his book *Jiai* was issued in 2004.

> until raised to Heaven
> I'll go to fields of green
> carrying my glove

昇天するまでグローブ抱え青野ゆく

shōten suru   made gurōbu kakae   aono yuku

beyond
the game of catch
drying seaweed

若布干すキャッチボールの向こう側
wakame hosu   kyatchi bōru no   mukou gawa

EXTRA

INNINGS

AMERICAN AND JAPANESE BASEBALL

Baseball in the United States

Baseball, America's national pastime, has a long tradition. The first organized game to closely resemble the modern one is generally recognized to have been played on June 19, 1846, in the Elysian Fields, a park along the Hudson River in Hoboken, New Jersey. That historic game was between the New York Knickerbockers and the New Yorks. Alexander Cartwright (1820–1892), a New York City fireman, has been called the inventor of baseball for creating the Knickerbockers (named for his Knickerbockers Engine Company of the New York City Fire Department), for writing the first rules, and for organizing that first game. He set the basis for the development of the modern game. Yet, evidence of forms of the game go much further back in time. The records of the Lewis and Clark expedition to the Northwest in 1804–1806 mention that the men on the expedition played a game of "base" with the Nez Percé Indians while they waited for the snows to melt on the Bitterroot Mountains before trying to cross them. It may have had some relation to what later became baseball. It's even possible that the game, at least in a primitive form, goes back to well before the American revolution.

Baseball spread rapidly from the New York area after the Knickerbockers were organized. First through the Northeast part of the country, then gradually South and West. During the Civil War, troops from the North introduced it to men from all over the country, even to rebel forces from the South. The first openly professional team was put together in 1869: the Cincinnati Red Stockings. After two years of barnstorming the country playing local teams, it moved to Boston and became part of the first professional baseball league formed in 1871.

Since then an almost religious reverence has grown up around baseball. It has become the most loved game in America. Just reciting the names of the legendary figures of professional baseball who helped to enshrine the game in the hearts of Americans can call up in our imaginations the feats they achieved. From the first five players named to the National Baseball Hall of Fame on its opening in 1939, Ty Cobb, Babe Ruth, Walter Johnson, Honus Wagner, and Christy Mathewson, to those who have joined them down through the years—and some who haven't—the names of these baseball giants ring out like magic bells calling up haiku-like images of the players in action: King Kelly (Slide Kelly, Slide); Tinker to Evers to Chance; Wee Willie Keeler (Hit 'Em Where They Ain't); "Shoeless" Joe Jackson; Tris Speaker; Jimmie Foxx; Lou Gehrig, the Iron Horse; Ted Williams, the Splendid Splinter; Joe DiMaggio, the Yankee Clipper; Hank Greenberg; Stan "The Man" Musial; Bob "Rapid Robert" Feller and Nolan Ryan; the "Say Hey Kid" Willie Mays; the Inscrutable Yogi Berra ("It Ain't Over Till It's Over"); Don Larsen; Jackie Robinson; Pee Wee Reese; Gil Hodges; Satchel "Don't Look Back" Paige, Walter Clemons; Henry "Hank" Aaron; Mickey Mantle and Roger Maris; Reggie Jackson; Rickey Henderson; and on and on.

Americans have remarkable champions to fill out their dream scorecards. Great hurlers and catchers, great infielders and outfielders, great batters and great base runners. And now they are being joined by great players from Japan, such as Hideki "Godzilla" Matsui with the Yankees and Ichiro Suzuki of the Mariners.

Baseball in Japan

Baseball was introduced to Japan in 1872 by Horace Wilson, an American teacher of mathematics and English at what is now Tokyo University. He was born in Gorham, Maine, on February 10, 1843, and died in San Francisco on March 4, 1927. Wilson arrived in Japan in 1871 and was a teacher at the school until 1877. He taught baseball to his students and colleagues and enjoyed playing the game with them. From there baseball spread to other schools and to amateur athletic clubs in the Tokyo area and then gradually to other parts of the country. Though there were a few professional baseball teams organized in the 1920s and early '30s, Major League Baseball didn't start in Japan until 1936. Today, besides the two major leagues (the Central and the Pacific Leagues), the pennant winners of which play each other in the Japan Series, there are two minor leagues that function as farm systems for the "majors" (NPB: Nippon Professional Baseball). Amateur baseball is still hugely popular with both students and the general population. University and high school teams compete in their own all-Japan championship tournaments, which are enthusiastically followed by the public and featured on national television.

The professional game from the beginning has been dominated by the Tokyo Yomiuri Giants of the Central League. Due to the wide coverage it gets from both television and other media (the team is owned by the *Yomiuri Shimbun,* one of Japan's biggest newspapers) and its ability to field outstanding teams, the Giants have been and continue to be the most popular baseball team in the country. They won nine Japan Series Championships in a row—from 1965 to 1973—and are as legendary in Japan as the New York Yankees are in the United States.

Sadaharu Oh, the Babe Ruth of Japan, hit 868 home runs during the twenty-two years (1959–80) he played for the Giants. More than either Babe Ruth or Hank Aaron. Oh also managed the Giants, winning one pennant in the five years he was at the helm (1984–88). Another Giants' player, Shigeo Nagashima, who played on the nine-in-a-row championship team, was the winner of six batting titles and is loved and revered in Japan as much as Joe DiMaggio is in the United States. Even earlier, Tetsuji Kawakami, a first baseman who wore glasses while playing, was a superstar for the Giants. His feats at the plate earned him the nickname, "God of Batting."

Baseball & Bēsubōru

Baseball is pronounced "bēsubōru" (baysubohru) in Japan. [The Japanese word yakyū also means baseball and tama asobi (playing with a ball) is sometimes translated as playing catch, or playing baseball.] Despite the similarity in the sounds of the words and though the Japanese game basically follows the same rules, there are important differences between the way baseball is played in Japan and the way it is played in America. In Japan the emphasis is on team spirit and harmony (*wa*), while a more individualistic spirit and a greater desire to shine as a star exist among American players. The stress on teamwork in Japan results in a slower style of play. There is more discussion between players and coaches during the game and more use of the bunt and the hit-and-run. Strategy is more important than just letting the player hit away, or letting him try to blast the ball out of the park. The result is that Japanese games tend to be three and four hours long.

Most Americans who have played in the Japanese system also think the Japanese teams tend to overtrain. This tendency comes from another Japanese moral ideal called *doryoku* (effort). It results in more strict discipline and the following of rigorous practice regimens on both the amateur and professional levels than one finds in the American game. Long and heavy workouts constantly take place in their training camps and during the regular season. The major league teams have both spring and autumn training camps, leaving the players with only one month, December, off each year. Added to this, they are often expected to arrive hours before each game for long practice sessions.

The tradition of Bushido, the way of the samurai warrior to unswervingly dedicate oneself to develop one's abilities to the utmost, enduring pain and privation to achieve perfection, has been adopted by coaches and players alike in Japanese baseball. When a Japanese pitcher feels his arm getting tired his manager will often tell him to keep on throwing to strengthen it while in America a pitcher will be advised to take it easy and to preserve his energy and strength by periodic rests. The Japanese coaches often expect players to practice until they are exhausted—the batter swings the bat a thousand times, the pitcher throws a thousand times—each player keeps on through pain and fatigue in an attempt to go beyond it, to work it out. This is one way he can fulfill the samurai ideals of *on* (obligation) and *giri* (duty) to his coach and his fellow players.

Zen, a Japanese form of Buddhism, which has been a

traditional part of the way of the samurai, has also been related to baseball. Kawakami, the "God of Batting," once said, "Bēsubōru is Zen." (R. H. Blyth, the great translator of haiku, wrote "Haiku is Zen.") The concentration of mind and the dedication to perfecting oneself that are part of Zen practice and meditation is seen as an aid in making one a better baseball player.

Since the interchange of players and coaches between the two countries in the last several decades and particularly with the popularity and success of such American players as Gregory "Boomer" Wells ("Boomah" was the triple-crown batting champ and MVP of the Pacific League in 1984) and Randy Bass (he took the triple crown and MVP in the Central League in 1985) playing for Japanese teams and Japanese stars like Ichiro Suzuki and Hideki Matsui playing in Major League Baseball in the United States the differences between the two styles of play are gradually changing. The Japanese are now seeing the wisdom of some system of rest while the Americans are seeing the advantages of tougher discipline and practice. The Japanese are seeing the excitement and enthusiasm that can be generated by a desire to excell as an individual as well as a team and American players are developing more of an appreciation for cultivating team spirit.

Of course these are generalizations and all types of play and practice, good or bad, can be found wherever the game is played. The history of the American game shows that there were many teams where the players put the team ahead of personal glory. For example, the championship teams of the New York Yankees in the late 1940s through the early '60s have been noted for their great teamwork. Yogi Berra, who won ten world series championship rings with those aggregations, has often remarked and written about how important team spirit was to the Yankees of that era. It was crucial in getting them to the top year after year. They had famous players—Joe DiMaggio, Mickey Mantle, and Yogi himself—but the team came first. And the Japanese game, while famous for team spirit, has been able to produce many outstanding individual stars, like Oh and Kawakami—and even a current Yankee, Hideki Matsui.

For a thorough history of Japanese baseball and how it differs from the American version of the game see Robert Whiting's *You Gotta Have Wa* (1989) and *The Meaning of Ichiro* (2004). Much if not most of the information on Japanese baseball appearing here was gleaned from these valuable sources. These books also chronicle in a vivid style and with fascinating detail the experiences of American players playing in the Japanese professional leagues and that of Japanese players playing for major league teams in the United States.

What both the Japanese and American players (and Canadians, Hispanics, Koreans, and other nationalities) share is a love for the game and a desire to perfect it in all of its manifestations. To execute with skill and art all aspects of the game: from pitching, batting, fielding, running the bases, and throwing, to game-winning strategies and tactics. And with all this, above all, to enjoy the game.

—Cor van den Heuvel
Spring 2006

195

BASEBALL & HAIKU BOOK LIST

Angell, Roger. *Once More Around the Park: A Baseball Reader*. New York: Ballantine Books, 1991. A prose writer with the haiku spirit, Angell knows how to get into the heart of baseball not only by getting to understand the players, but through the vividly evoked action of the games, their settings, and even the players' equipment—there is an essay about the ball itself. This and his *Game Time: A Baseball Companion* (2003) bring together some of his best work.

Arima Akito. *Einstein's Century: Akito Arima's Haiku*, translations by Emiko Miyashita & Lee Gurga. Decatur, Illinois: Brooks Books, 2001. Fine translations along with valuable introductions by William J. Higginson and the translators. No baseball haiku.

Beichman, Janine. *Masaoka Shiki*. Boston: Twayne Publishers, 1982. Best book in English on Shiki. Includes a discussion of one of his baseball tanka, but does not mention his baseball haiku.

Blyth, R. H. *Haiku*. Tokyo: Hokuseido Press, 1949–52. 4 vols. No baseball in this or his other books.
———. *A History of Haiku*. Tokyo: Hokuseido Press, 1963–64. 2 vols.
———. *Japanese Life and Character in Senryu*. Tokyo: Hokuseido Press, 1960.

Brooks, Randy M., and Lee Gurga, eds. *Midwest Haiku Anthology*. Decatur, Illinois: High/Coo Press (now Brooks Books), 1992.

Dickson, Paul. *The Dickson Baseball Dictionary*. New York: Facts on File, 1989. A valuable resource for the baseball writer in any genre and for the player or fan who wants to know the game's terminology and how it's been used through the years.

Hall, Donald. *Fathers Playing Catch with Sons: Essays on Sport [Mostly Baseball]*. New York: North Point Press, 1985. The poet with the lean and up-close prose about base-ball. Has interesting history of writings on the game: prose and poetry, fact and fiction.

Henderson, Harold G. *An Introduction to Haiku*. Garden City, New York: Doubleday & Company, 1958.

Higginson, William J. *Haiku World: An International Poetry Almanac*. Tokyo: Kodansha International, 1996. A rare example of an English-language saijiki, or haiku almanac, a type of book that is very common in Japan. Over one thou-sand haiku in twenty-five languages from around the world with English translations. Includes only two baseball haiku: David Elliott's "Night game" and Bud Goodrich's "Squeeze play," which are also in this anthology. Has lists of season words for each season with examples of haiku using them. This and his *The Haiku Seasons* (1996) show how closely haiku and the seasons are connected.

Kacian, Jim, and Cor van den Heuvel, eds. *Past Time*. Winchester, Virginia: Red Moon Press, 1999. Thirty-one haiku poets each contributed one baseball haiku to this out-of-print chapbook, which, along with a companion chapbook *Play Ball* (baseball haiku by Cor van den Heuvel), was the inspiration for the present anthology.

Katō Kōko. *A Hidden Pond: Anthology of Modern Haiku,* edited by Kōko Katō, translated with commentary by Kōko Katō and David Burleigh. Tokyo: Kadokawa Shoten, 1997. Best collection of modern and contemporary Japanese haiku in English. Includes original Japanese and *romaji* (Romanized spelling of Japanese language) transliterations. Excellent translations and superb commentaries. No baseball haiku.

Kerouac, Jack. *Book of Haikus,* edited by Regina Weinreich. New York: Penguin, 2003. Kerouac was the first American to write a baseball haiku. This book includes not only his two baseball haiku, but nearly all the haiku (over five hundred) he ever wrote—good and bad. With a fine introduction by the editor.

Masaoka Shiki. *Selected Poems,* translated by Burton Watson. New York: Columbia University Press, 1997. Good translations. Has romaji transliterations, but not the original Japanese. Includes one of Shiki's nine baseball haiku.
———. *If Someone Asks... Masaoka Shiki's Life and Haiku,* translations by The Shiki-Kinen Museum English Volunteers. Matsuyama, Ehime: The Matsuyama Municipal Shiki-Kinen Museum, 2001. One hundred and sixteen of Shiki's haiku in the original Japanese, with romanized versions, English translations, and commentaries. Includes two of his baseball haiku: "spring breeze– / the green field /

tempts me to play catch" and "lush grass / the baseball path / is white."

Matsuyama Municipal Shiki-Kinen Museum. *Shiki and Matsuyama*. No author given. English edition edited and translated by Ruth S. McCreery. Matsuyama, Ehime: The Matsuyama Municipal Shiki-Kinen Museum, 1986. Contains what may be the first publication in a book of one of Shiki's baseball haiku in English translation: "To be young! / Children gather / to hit a ball."

Ozaki Hosai. *Right Under the Big Sky, I Don't Wear a Hat: The Haiku and Prose of Hōsai Ozaki,* translated by Hiroaki Sato. Berkeley, California: Stone Bridge Press, 1993. Great book by one of the most important modern free-form haiku poets. Outstanding translations.

Rielly, Edward J. "Baseball Haiku: Bashō, the Babe, and the Great Japanese-American Trade," in *The Cooperstown Symposium on Baseball and American Culture, 2001,* edited by William M. Simons. Jefferson, North Carolina: McFarland, 2002. Pages 246–59. What baseball and haiku have in common. Superb, groundbreaking article on baseball haiku.

Ross, Bruce, ed. *Haiku Moment: An Anthology of Contemporary North American Haiku.* Boston, Rutland, Vermont, & Tokyo: Charles E. Tuttle Company, 1993. Widely representative collection of the conventional haiku mainstream. No baseball haiku.

Takaha Shugyo. *Selected Haiku,* edited and translated by Hoshino Tsunehiko and Adrian Pinnington with an introduction by Hoshino Tsunehiko. Tokyo: Furansudo, 2003.

Takaha writes some of the very best contemporary Japanese haiku. They are presented here in splendid translations. No baseball haiku.

Swede, George, and Randy Brooks, eds. *Global Haiku: Twenty-five Poets World-wide.* Oakville, Ontario, and Niagara Falls, New York: Mosaic Press, 2000. Haiku by prominent English-language poets from around the world. Includes two baseball haiku: Bill Pauly's "country field" and an early version of Cor van den Heuvel's "the batter checks."

Ueda, Makoto, ed. and trans. *Modern Japanese Haiku: An Anthology.* Toronto: University of Toronto Press, 1976. Especially valuable for having the original Japanese, romaji transliterations, and literal translations for each word as well as decent literary translations. Has an important introduction that details the different schools of haiku after Shiki and how they determined the paths taken by modern Japanese haiku. It has one baseball haiku by Saitō Sanki, which we quote here (in our translation) in Akimoto Fujio's profile.

van den Heuvel, Cor, ed. *The Haiku Anthology: Haiku and Senryu in English.* New York: W. W. Norton & Company, 1999. The celebrated third edition.

Whiting, Robert. *The Meaning of Ichiro: The New Wave from Japan and the Transformation of Our National Pastime.* New York: Warner Books, 2004. How Japanese baseball stars such as Ichiro Suzuki and Hideki Matsui playing in the American major leagues are helping to change baseball in the United States. This and Whiting's earlier book *You*

Gotta Have Wa (1989), which recounts the history and describes the spirit of Japanese baseball (while also detailing the role of American players in the Japanese majors), will tell you everything you ever wanted to know about the similarities and differences between Japanese and American baseball.

Wong, Stephen. (With photographs by Susan Einstein). *Smithsonian Baseball: Inside the World's Finest Private Collections.* New York: HarperCollins, 2005. The artifacts of the game preserved by collectors. From famous players' equipment (gloves, balls, bats, uniforms, etc.) to baseball cards, vintage photographs, posters, awards, scorecards, and just about any object that can be connected to the game are presented here in beautifully designed photographic layouts and fascinatingly detailed text. The stuff of a haiku poet's (or any baseball fan's) dreams.

Yamaguchi Seishi. *The Essence of Modern Haiku: 300 Poems by Seishi Yamaguchi,* translated by Takashi Kodaira and Alfred Marks. Marietta, Florida: Mangajin, Inc., 1993. The translations are a bit stilted and padded to get the poems into the five-seven-five form in English, but the translators include literal translations of the key words in each haiku so readers can fashion their own translations. Also contains both the original Japanese and romaji transliterations. A valuable addition: Seishi's own comments on each haiku with the date and circumstances that inspired them. Two of his baseball haiku (also in this book) are included.

INDEX OF POETS

Americans

Japanese

ACKNOWLEDGMENTS

The editors thank the following poets, magazines, and publishers for permission to print these poems:

(Note: Every effort has been made to contact copyright holders; the editors would be pleased to hear from any copyright holders not acknowledged below. The copyright for previously unpublished poems reverts to the authors of the poems. The poems of Masaoka Shiki, Kawahigashi Hekigotō, and Ozawa Seiyūshi are according to the Berne Convention no longer protected by copyright, but the Japanese sources for the poems are included here. Japanese names are listed in the Japanese manner, family name first.)

Akimoto Fujio: "in the far sky" from *Manza,* Kadokawa Shoten, Tokyo, copyright © 1967 by Akimoto Fujio; by permission of the Japan Writers Association.

Arima Akito: "Kōshien Stadium" from *Fuki* (*Not Exceptional*), Kadokawa Shoten, Tokyo, copyright © 2004 by Arima Akito; by permission of the author.

Randy Brooks: "opening day" from *Past Time,* Red Moon Press, Winchester, Virginia, copyright © 1999 by Randy Brooks; all other poems (four) previously unpublished; by permission of the author.

Tom Clausen: "in the shoe box" from *Bases Loaded,* a

Sylvia Forges-Ryan: "waiting to bat" and "rained out" from *Fan* magazine, "Special Baseball Haiku Issue" (1998), copyright © 1998 by Sylvia Forges-Ryan; "sandlot players" previously unpublished; by permission of the author.

Brenda Gannam: all nine poems previously unpublished; by permission of the author.

David Giacalone: "squinting to see him" from *Roadrunner Haiku Journal,* vol. 5, no. 4, November 2005; "law office picnic" previously unpublished; by permission of the author.

Arthur "Bud" Goodrich: all seven poems from *Rhubarb! The Collected Senryu and Haiku of Bud Goodrich,* Deep North Press, Evanston, Illinois, copyright © 2003 by Arthur Goodrich; by permission of the author.

Lee Gurga: "rumble of thunder" from *Too Busy for Spring,* 1999 HNA Anthology, edited by Michael Dylan Welch and Lee Gurga, Press Here, Foster City, California, copyright © 1999 by Lee Gurga; all other poems (four) previously unpublished; by permission of the author.

Hoshino Tsunehiko: "my son runs toward" from *Ten (Marten)* haiku magazine, copyright © by Hoshino Tsunehiko; by permission of the author.

Imai Sei: "the baseball stadium's" from *Hokugen (Northern Limit),* Bokuyosha, Tokyo, copyright © 1984 by Imai Sei; all other poems (eight) from *Tanima no Kagu (The Valley's Furniture),* Kadakawa Shoten, Tokyo, copyright © 2000 by Imai Sei; by permission of the author.

Jim Kacian: "calm evening" from *Past Time,* Red Moon Press, Winchester, Virginia, copyright © 1999 by Jim Kacian; "October revival" from the *Piedmont Literary Review* (circa 1992) © Jim Kacian; all other poems (three) previously unpublished; by permission of the author.

Kadokawa Genyoshi: "lights-out siren" from *Saigyō no*

from *Acorn,* copyright © 2005 by Ed Markowski; all other poems (thirteen) previously unpublished; by permission of the author.

Masaoka Shiki: all nine poems from *Shiki Zenshū* (*The Complete Works of Shiki*), Masaoka Chuuzaburoo, et al., eds., Kodansha, Tokyo 1975–1978.

Dan McCullough: "entering" from *Frogpond,* vol. 27, no. 3, copyright © 2004 by Dan McCullough; "darkening clouds" from *Frogpond,* vol. 25, no. 2, copyright © 2002 by Dan McCullough; "shooting star" from *Modern Haiku,* vol. 35, no. 1, copyright © 2004 by Dan McCullough; all other poems (six) previously unpublished; by permisssion of the author.

Mizuhara Shūōshi: "night game" from *Banka* (*Late Flowers*); "a night game's" from *Ryoshū* (*Travel Tedium*); "[Five] Scenes at Jingu Baseball Stadium" from *Shūōshi Kushū* (*Shūōshi's Collected Haiku*); all copyright © Mizuhara Shūōshi; by permission of Mizuhara Haruo.

Ozawa Seiyūshi: "the autumn sky" from the *Gendai Haiku Senshū* (*Modern Haiku Anthology*), 1941.

Tom Painting: "all day rain" and "bases loaded" from *piano practice,* Bottle Rockets Press, Wethersfield, Connecticut, copyright © 2004 by Tom Painting; "the foul ball lands" from *Modern Haiku,* vol. 35, no. 2, copyright © 2004 by Tom Painting; by permission of the author.

Bill Pauly: "country field" from *Past Time,* Red Moon Press, Winchester, Virginia, copyright © 1999 by Bill Pauly; all other poems (four) previously unpublished; by permission of the author.

Alan Pizzarelli: "at the produce stand," "the score keeper," and "saturday afternoon" from *The Windswept Corner,* Bottle Rockets Press, Wethersfield, Connecticut, copyright © 2005 by Alan Pizzarelli; "at shortstop" from